from the Banks of the Nile

to the Shores of the Great Lakes

The author, in her home in Wisconsin.

from the
Banks of the Nile
to the
Shores of the Great Lakes

Mary Nessim Khair

Celo Valley Books
Burnsville, North Carolina

Copies of this book may be obtained by sending to the publisher for each copy:
U.S. orders: $18.95 + $3.00 shipping/handling
Canadian orders: $25.95 + $5.50 shipping/handling

This book was designed and produced by
Celo Book Production Service
346 Seven Mile Ridge Road
Burnsville NC 28714

ISBN 0-923687-46-7
Library of Congress Catalog Card Number 97-77838

Copyright © 1998 by Mary Nessim Khair
All rights reserved.
Printed in the United States of America

No part of this book may be reproduced or transmitted in any form or by any means, electronic or mechanical, including photocopying, recording, or by any information storage and retrieval system, without permission in writing from the publisher, except short excerpts used in reviews, in which full publishing information is given.

For my daughters,
Carmen Mary and Nancy Isis Khair

So long as men can breathe, or eyes can see,
So long lives this, and this gives life to thee.
—William Shakespeare, "Sonnet XVIII"

Contents

Acknowledgments xi

1 Arriving in New York City 1

2 My First Two Years in the USA 21

3 Moving to New England 37

4 Leaving the East Coast for the Midwest 55

5 Living as a U.S. Citizen 69

6 Life in Egypt under Nasser 89

7 Teenage Years and Father's Death 105

8 College, Trips, and Riots 121

9 Work in England, Returning
   to Egypt, and the Wedding 135

Poems 149

Recipes from Egypt 165

Acknowledgments

My gratitude to Professor William Harrold, of the English department at the University of Wisconsin–Milwaukee, is greater than words on this page can hold. He welcomed my project with his usual interest, enthusiasm, patience, limitless advice, and helpful step-by-step directions as the book was taking shape. Every time I called on him from underwater, regardless of how busy he was, he lent an ear and then shed light on the best direction to take.

Thank you, Carmen, for proofreading; Nancy, for your continued confidence and encouragement; and Gamil, for giving me the opportunity to carry out my writing.

I am very grateful to Carolyn Mitchell and every member of Cheney Travel, for helping me with my work so that I could concentrate on my writing as I wished.

Thank you, Lynda Rickun, not only for the time you gave me, but for your encouragement and interest in my work.

Thank you, Father Rewis Awadalla, for clarifying and revising the information regarding the Coptic Orthodox Church traditions, for encouraging me, and for your confidence in me.

Thank you, Carol Banoub and family, for opening the doors of opportunity for me with such love and enthusiasm, as well as for cheering me on all the time.

Thank you to all the Egyptian community in Milwaukee for your love and encouragement.

To my special friends in Mequon and those who moved out of state, who supported, listened, and were in attendance when I read my poetry or spoke about my literary projects, I am forever grateful for your loving interest.

To Martin Norden and Sharon Devries, I extend my heartfelt gratitude for your help and encouragement.

To my editor, Diana Donovan, at Celo Valley Books, for her help, cooperation, attention to detail, accuracy, and most of all for handling my work so gently, thus eliminating all my worries regarding publishing my book.

At this point I will extend my thanks across the Atlantic and beyond to thank my mother, sisters, brother, and my nieces and nephews who are so proud of me. All your letters and phone calls gave me the energy to continue writing.

Much of the material on Egypt under Nasser in chapter eight was checked against facts given in Robert Stephens's *Nasser: A Political Biography* (New York: Simon and Schuster, 1971).

1
Arriving in New York City

"Okay," I once said to my schoolteacher as a child at English Mission College in Cairo, Egypt, in mid-1950s.

"Don't say okay. That is American usage. Write two hundred lines of 'I must not say okay.' We are learning English here, for that is the use of the language you will most likely need when you are an adult."

Little had we known that this would not turn out to be the case for me.

English Mission College, which had grades kindergarten through twelve, was built in Cairo for the children of the British diplomats and dignitaries during the colonization of Egypt. In the mid-1950s the school was still British run, and it still educated its pupils as if they were in England.

I was the youngest of the four children of the Rizk family. My parents, like several other Egyptian families, were keen on giving each of us the best education offered in the land. My father's job with the Egyptian government provided the income to pay the bills. And my older brother and my two older sisters had certainly shown more than enough intelligence there to make them acceptable to English Mission College.

In the shadow of their good reputations, haunted by childhood allergies, I too attended, though I did not feel myself to be as gifted as they. I studied hard. If I did well, the teachers took it for granted because I belonged to the Rizk family; if my performance was poor, I was excused because of my health.

But of the four of us it was I who would need to learn the American uses of the English language, as well as American customs. For after finishing at English Mission College, and going on to get my B.A. degree in English literature at Ain Shams University, I found myself marrying, in 1969, Gamil Khair, an Egyptian medical doctor in training, who was to finish his internship in Brooklyn, New York.

I had been to England twice on short trips, to visit my sister Isis and my brother Samir, both doctors there. There, I had been able to indulge my love for travel and I had seen the country, first through my expectations, which had been built up over the years as I read the stories of English authors, and then through my own experiences there. But the United States was not a place I ever really thought I'd see, as it was so far from Egypt, geographically, culturally, and politically.

Life often hands us what we least expect, doesn't it? In September 1969, at the age of twenty-two, having read a few American novels and seen a few American movies, I traveled from my home in Cairo, to England, then on to the United States with my dreams intact of what life in America would be.

Coming from a country with over five *thousand* years of history to a country (at that time) under two *hundred* years of age, I thought everything would be new. I was used to seeing very old buildings in Egypt, but I did not expect this to be true in America. I thought I would be seeing only fancy ones, like the ones in Hollywood movies. I expected to see streets shining like an ice rink before a big show, but planted with trees and flowers. I thought the buses, trains, subways, and cars would be as new as next year's model Cadillac, and as quiet. I was sure all the houses would be copies of the White House. Hollywood and fiction had not prepared me for the boroughs of New York.

I landed with Gamil at JFK International Airport on September 4, 1969. The very first people I saw when I stepped out of Customs were the teenagers of the 1960s, wearing torn shorts and patched jeans and displaying messy hair and dirty fingernails. I was shocked, then saddened. I felt cheated of my dreams.

In Egypt, though my own family was fairly well off, I had seen my country torn by war and poverty. I had wanted to take advantage of the best in life, to improve my station in life. My friends and I had gone to the beautician regularly, and we dressed according to the styles dictated by the fashion houses of European designers. Knowing that the United States had not had a war in over a hundred years, I had naturally thought Americans would want to be even more elegant than we Egyptians. Why, in such a rich and new country, would people choose a look like that of these teens? What could it all mean?

With these questions in my mind, I followed my husband outside the terminal, to a line of people waiting for taxis to take them into the city. It was clear to me that the challenges of the next few years would be more than what I had thought they would be. I felt overwhelmed by the new beginnings I faced.

I had been prepared for my new life as a married woman, with all the new responsibilities such a life entailed, so different from those of a student—responsibilities to be faced without a mother or sister or close friend nearby. And this learning how to live in a new country—I had thought of it as a gentle form of exile. But now I saw how radically different people here dressed, and I wondered how I appeared to them—out of place? The weather, too, was a factor I'd have to deal with: the humid heat of late summer, I knew, would not last here. I wondered how one dressed for New York winters. The New York City system of transportation was daunting too. I could see, as we stood in the long taxi line outside the terminal, that traveling within the city would take some learning.

A bride of eight days, I stood in that line for what seemed like hours, surrounded by the noise and fumes of jet engines, trucks, cars, and buses, waiting our turn for a Yellow Cab. The man organizing the procedure flagged cabs and shoved people into them frantically, allowing no disagreements from passengers or cab drivers. But each time he said he had a couple to go to

Brooklyn, the cabbie shook his head, and we were told to stand aside and let the next person, going somewhere else, take that ride. We were extremely tired after a long flight crossing the Atlantic, and we were new enough that we had no appreciation of a cab driver's point of view: Brooklyn is not laid out like Manhattan and Queens, with their grids of easily found numbered streets and avenues. Brooklyn meanders in and out, around a few long parkways. Cab drivers unfamiliar with Brooklyn easily get lost, and when this happens on the return trip, this costs them a lot in lost wages.

Bewildered, we waited. When we finally were given the nod of approval, however reluctantly, by a cab driver, I was relieved. The relief, however, was not to be for long.

We fell into a very uncomfortable backseat that was efficient at transferring each bump in the road directly into our bodies. Either the seat springs had lost their spring or the cab needed new shock absorbers. I looked at Gamil, but he was very tired and fed up. I wanted very much to say something, to ask the cab driver to slow down so that we would at least not be jostled so harshly, but I didn't have to. The cab driver was pulling over to the side of the road.

He called out to another cab, coming from the opposite direction, and asked us to switch taxis as he, like the others, did not really want to drive us to Brooklyn. This other driver, we were told, was a native of Brooklyn, so he knew his way around. His cab was also, it turned out, more comfortable.

The houses we passed, and the apartment buildings, were not new. Nor were the streets shining. Finally we arrived at our destination, 122 Ashland Place, Brooklyn, New York.

Gamil pointed the apartment building out to me. It was a high-rise red brick building lacking beauty or personality. Sixteen stories high, there was garbage piled on the side of the entrance. The hospital was across the street from the front side of the building, but our apartment was overlooking the back, where an open parking lot was between our building and the identical one next to it. Even though Gamil was pointing out the entrance to the hospital, I was too absorbed looking at the place where we were to live, trying to find something to like about it. I was not impressed by its appearance or its location, which lacked cleanliness and safety.

We got on the elevator, after checking in at the front desk. Our apartment was on the fifteenth floor, but the numbers for the floors, displayed in the elevator car, went from twelve to fourteen, then on to fifteen. I asked Gamil if he knew why this was. He said the thirteenth floor is always skipped because people here were superstitious—they won't rent apartments on the thirteenth floor.

Once again, the same feeling of disappointment that I'd felt earlier, at the airport, returned. Superstition? I had always thought it was a thing of the past, like myth.

When we arrived at the furnished apartment that was to be ours and opened the door, I saw that there would be a great deal of work waiting for me. There were cartons filled with china and other household goods and there were empty cabinets just waiting to be filled. My husband had worked industriously on the apartment in his free time, as he had been interning in the States for the whole previous year, living in the doctors' residence for that hospital in the Bronx until June 1969, then at the apartment here in Brooklyn. He had hung some wallpaper, in an attempt to make the place livable. He had even shopped for linens, silverware, and more, before going to Egypt for our wedding.

But even with all this, I was disappointed that the giant building was an old one, and that this apartment where we would begin our new life together was furnished with old furniture, some of which was broken. There were no pots or pans in the kitchen yet, which meant no cooking. We would have to go out for every meal, including breakfast—which would have been fine had I known how to eat a stack of pancakes!

My first breakfast meal was just that. I watched with fascination as other people spread the butter between each layer of the several thick pancakes on their plates, poured the syrup, cut, and ate. In Egypt, when we prepared pancakes, they were not these thick cakes. They were the thin, delicately rolled pastries filled with fruit or cheese, which I later found to be called crêpes here. (I now prepare American-style pancakes for my children's breakfast as if I've known how to do so all my life.)

Thank goodness, reading and speaking basic English were not problems I had to deal with. I could read the paper and the signs on the street, watch TV, talk to salespeople, answer the phone, and follow most of what people were saying. At first, though, the difference between my English accent and their American one made it difficult sometimes for people to understand me totally, and for me to perceive all they were saying to me.

After breakfast at the nearest restaurant, that first morning in the United States, we went to catch the subway to go to the bank in Manhattan. Having used the Underground in London, where the seats are covered with velour and the trains run smoothly and quietly, I expected America's subways to run even more smoothly and to be lined, maybe, with silk or velvet rather than velour.

After a few minutes of waiting in the dull, dark DeKalb subway station, I heard a screech. I ground my teeth and shook my shoulders, but my ears remained deafened for a second or two. A cold wind blew into my face, and a dimly lit, brown, dingy train arrived. The doors opened and we climbed in. The train took off with another screech.

The seats were wooden and there was a hole in the floor showing the tracks. I was reminded of the trains in old cowboy films. *Is this an antique? The very first train ever to run in America?* I asked myself. *Or is it just my luck that the first train I get on is one of the oldest and most decrepit in the city?*

When we switched trains to continue our journey, the answer became apparent. The other trains were still noisy, but the seats were made out of some kind of metal, and at least they were newer, brighter, and more cheerful.

After we bought pots and pans for the kitchen, we found out that the oven in our apartment was not working. Even with Gamil's year in the United States, we were not aware that we could simply report the malfunction to the manager and wait for it to be repaired. In Egypt, when you rent an apartment—which is the most common way of living—the owner of the building is not responsible for the apartment's contents. There were no furnished apartments either, when I lived there. All the furnishings of the apartment, including the major appliances like stove and refrigerator, belonged to the tenants; they were responsible for replacement, purchase, and repair. So when we found that the oven was not working, we naturally bought a new one.

Though we could have saved the money by asking the manager of our building to repair the old one, at least we now had the ability to cook our own meals. We were finally ready to start making our first home together in the United States of America.

There were other Egyptian immigrants living around the city —some in Queens, others in New Jersey. They gathered on Saturdays, when a priest—Father Roufail Younan—came all the way from Montreal, Canada, to conduct Mass. (Toronto is where the first Coptic Orthodox church was built in North America, and the priest serving there was Father Marcos Marcos.) This small group of Egyptian Christians rented a church to pray in their traditional ways: in Arabic and Coptic, and using the longer, more elaborate Coptic rites. (Coptic is an ancient language used for prayer in our church, in the same way that Latin is used in the Roman rite.)

We gathered after prayer to talk about the future, the past; about the old and the new; and about the good and bad that we were experiencing as a result of our choice to leave our home country and immigrate. We spoke in our mother tongue, the Arabic language; we joked, laughed, cried, and complained to each other. Together, we were like one family in a strange place, even though we really were strangers to each other, and hadn't known each other before leaving Egypt and landing in New York. We were united in one language, religion, similar background, ambition, and adventure. It was a fine and friendly group of people.

When the United States opens its doors for immigration in a country, it specifies the professions it will accept. When this happened for Egypt in the 1960s, the request was for medical doctors, engineers, architects, and accountants.

I was thinking of my future, of jobs and of continuing my graduate education, so I asked for the advice of the people who were here before me to learn how to go about planning what to do with myself. Going to New York University for a master's in English literature was my goal at the time, since I had just completed my B.A. in that field, in Egypt before getting married and leaving home. One of the women talked me out of it.

She said that I should put my B.A. in English on the shelf "to collect dust" and forget about it. I should start a "more useful career." Her words caused me intense distress: creative arts helped me see the light and the world; literature nourished me, for through literature I had learned about some of my fellow human beings living in other parts of the globe. But I thought about what she said.

She was believed to be a very well-informed person. In Egypt this lady and her sister were known for their theological writing. In New York she worked for New York University's library, and her husband was an engineer. Her point of view in advising me was that I would never be able to make a career in English literature in a country where the first language is English and my mother tongue is not English. I was convinced, though saddened.

"Shorthand and typing" was her advice for me. "That's how you can get a job." I had always disliked secretarial work; I like creativity, not dictated ideas. I felt as if the doors were being closed firmly in front of me as far as a career choice went. It was true that shorthand and typing would help me down the road, but I could not settle for this choice as a career. I was sure there had to be something better.

I learned that the way to find a school to attend to learn a skill was to look up the names of schools in a book called the "yellow pages," and so I did. The last week in October, six weeks after I arrived in the States, I started classes at Taylor School of Business, in Manhattan, on Forty-second Street between the Avenue of the Americas and Fifth Avenue. Students were to pay three hundred dollars and the result was, they said, guaranteed. They promised that in eight weeks the student would be able to take dictation at the speed of one hundred and twenty words per minute in speedwriting, and type fifty words a minute.

Our group of students was a mixture ranging in age from the teens to people who were retired and learning a new skill. There were various nationalities: besides Americans, some came from South America, India, Italy—and even this one Egyptian student. The teaching technique was different from the high-school typing I had taken. Even opening a locker was a different experience. The combination locker was more like a little magic show for me. I shared one with an American student of Spanish descent; we attended the same classes and courses. We became good friends, perhaps because her parents were Spanish and she was familiar with the Mediterranean ways of thinking and dealing with people and situations. I also made friends with a Brazilian American young woman whose boyfriend was in Vietnam with the American army. I felt a certain sense of familiarity when I spoke with her; memories of the wars I had lived through came to mind.

I thought about the two wars I went through while in Egypt. One in 1956, the second in 1967, only two years before I arrived in New York. The 1956 attack on Egypt by the three countries England, France, and Israel occurred when Nasser nationalized the Suez Canal; the Six-Day War with Israel in 1967 was a major setback for Egypt, in which it lost some of its eastern territory.

My feelings of sadness for those who were giving up their young lives, of anger at those responsible for making wars and for the tearing up and the suffering of families, and of gloom brought on by the very subject of war—all this was very fresh in my memory. I didn't know if I felt more sorry for her or for her boyfriend and his family. I expressed these feelings as best as I could in the following poem:

> WAR
>
> Friend of the Devil,
> Lover of hate:
> Thunder, your music,
> Darkness, your shelter,
> Destruction, your motto,
> Maiming, your sport.
>
> Separator of lovers,
> Imposer of misery,
> Generator of fear,
> Child orphanager,
> Mothers' torturer
> Fathers' sorrow:
> To the news of death you rejoice,
> To the moans of mourning you dance.

In spite of the memories my friendship with the Brazilian American young woman brought to mind, I continued to be her friend during my unhappy stay at the Taylor School of Business.

My feelings about typing and shorthand did not get any better. I felt stuck in this place but had to complete the courses. The school was open-after hours for those students who wanted to stay and practice their typing or take dictation. There were tapes running all the time at different levels of speed for the students to train.

One evening, I stayed after school to do some extra typing. A student asked the teacher in charge a question about the typing she was working on. The teacher looked at her watch and said, "It's four-thirty-five, I'm only paid till four-thirty. You can ask me this question tomorrow." I stopped my typing for a second, trying to absorb the answer. If I had been in this student's place I would have felt like I'd been hit by a rock.

That year, (1969–1970), there were bomb scares every now and then in New York and all over the United States. People were protesting the unfairness of the Vietnam War, and one way some expressed their discontent was by planting bombs in places least suspected. Once there was one in a coat pocket at Macy's department store. Another bomb scare was at the school of business where I was attending my courses. The entire second floor was vacated, but not the third where we were.

I was disturbed. I couldn't decide whether to stay or to leave. Some students left, others were very calm about it. I went to get my coat and began watching and trying to decide whether to leave or not. I thought, *During wars, one knows that an underground shelter is the safest place to be, but what do you do in a case where you don't know what to expect?*

While I was standing there, debating in my own mind whether to stay or to leave, a student in the dictation room looked at me and said, "What are you carrying your coat for? Sit down and take some dictation. If it doesn't get you here, it will get you on the subway." Her words made sense. I hung up my coat and sat down to take some dictation practice. Soon after, the police came by our classroom and announced that the bomb scare was a false alarm!

As for the courses in speedwriting and typing, I thought I had a good enough background in the English language to get me through without too much trouble. Well, I was wrong.

Speedwriting was an obstacle. Students had to take a test in both classes every week. I did well enough in my typing course, but when it came to speedwriting, I did not do well. We took the first test where we had to pass taking dictation at a speed of sixty words per minute, transcribe it, and after a four-week intensive course of learning about the rules, exceptions, and abbreviations, we would take the exam. I failed.

I could take down the dictation but I could not make sense out of the sentences I'd written in order to transcribe them. It took me the longest time to realize that my problem was the difference in pronunciation between American and British speakers. Vowels, for one thing. Also, the soft American *t* sound vanished for me when a person spoke quickly. An example of this is as follows. For:

"Our plant in New Haven is ready to handle your order."

I was hearing and transcribing:

"Our plan in New Haven is ready to handle your order."

Or for:

"We can't ship your order on that date."

I would hear and transcribe:

"We can ship your order on that date."

Mistakes like this would cause disaster in the workplace and they led my teacher to believe I didn't understand English. This caused me a great deal of frustration, and a loss of hope that I would ever find a career for myself in the United States.

In conjunction with the above problem, I had another one with regional accents. I did not know that New York black people pronounced some words differently from white people, and our teacher was black. I missed my first test trying to figure out where the *x* came from in the sentence "Tom axed his boss for a raise."

A split-second hesitation while taking dictation throws the whole idea of "speedwriting" out the window. I finally made it through the sixty-word-per-minute test after a few tries, and moved on to the eighty-words-per-minute. However, to start the eighty, I had to move to another class, one taught by a white teacher with a more familiar accent. Having gotten used to the black teacher's dictation, I had to start all over again. What was supposed to have taken eight weeks, took nine *months* for me, and graduation was not easy.

I did not let school discourage me totally. Before completing the course I started looking for work. I decided to apply for a job at the United Nations—perhaps some translation between English and Arabic, or maybe some typing.

I took the subway to the giant building, and went up to the thirty-fifth floor, where Personnel was. Just having the opportunity to go there and fill out an application seemed like an uplifting experience to me. I was given an appointment for a test, and I left the building with my spirits soaring as high as my body had been.

When the day for my test came, I went back to the U.N. building and to the thirty-fifth floor once again. I was led to a huge room full of people there to take the same test. I did not know anyone, and that was an unsettling feeling. I looked around, and assumed that these other people all had experience in the business world. I had none whatsoever, except for a few weeks at a company in England, where I had worked while visiting my sister. I had never taken a test for a job, and I hadn't even graduated yet from Taylor School of Business. I lost any trace of self-confidence. I began to feel as small as an ant at the base of a mountain.

A sheet of paper filled with more than sixty questions was distributed. It was coated with something glossy, and it glared under the fluorescent lights, making it difficult to read. The questions were amusing; smart, very clever. I had never come across anything like them in my entire life at school, college, or anywhere. I was told later that it was an aptitude test.

I sat back and read the questions, enjoyed them, and admired the brains of those who had thought them up. I did not realize that I was supposed to answer them in a given amount of time. I could have spent all day reading and enjoying them over and over, but the examiner started the countdown. When the answers were collected, I had answered only two or three of them.

Then came the typing test. I was seated at a typewriter, given a sheet of paper on which to type, and another one to copy from. I did not check the typewriter, believing that all the typewriters would be the same. I began to type at my highest speed, which at that time was already fifty words per minute. I finished in good time, pulled my paper out of the machine—and nearly collapsed. It looked most peculiar. Where had all those reversed question marks come from? All those accents on or between letters? I knew I was much better than that in typing and could not have made errors like those. I looked at the keyboard. It puzzled me. I found out later that I had been seated at a Spanish typewriter.

All the examinees were asked to sit in the hall and wait for the results of the test. Why did I even wait? Well, I guess I just wanted to enjoy every minute I could in that building; I knew the result right there and then, but I chose to stay and hear it straight from the office. I was called in, when it was my turn, and told very politely that I did not make it. I got on the elevator and went down the thirty-five floors, my spirits sinking with me.

In the meantime, the Egyptian community was continuing to grow. We bought a small church in New Jersey, and our Pope in Egypt ordained a priest, Father Ghobrial Amin, to serve the Christian Egyptian population in the area. That was where we went each Sunday to pray and to meet our new friends. One Sunday I met a young man whose parents had been my parents' good friends for many years. It was as if I were finding a long-lost companion in the middle of a deserted island, and he felt the same way. We had attended the same school in Egypt, English Mission College, so we started talking with each other about how different it is to listen and speak to Americans and how much we missed out on meanings and words because of the different accents. We both felt much better about ourselves as we discussed this because, individually, we had each doubted our own strength and knowledge of the language. Finding someone else in the same boat made me feel much better.

I continued to go to the business school to complete my speedwriting course, and was also looking for a job. Every job I applied for, I was given an aptitude test. I became very familiar with those questions, as most of them were either the same or similar. I still thought it was very clever of whoever thought up those questions and put them together to quiz people like me. The difference was that by then I was answering them as soon as I received them in my hand. At some of the places where I applied for a job, such as at a firm on Wall Street, I felt I did not belong, and I found myself asking myself, *Why am I here? What am I doing here? I don't know anything about Wall Street: how it functions, what it stands for, what its history is.* I took a good look around at the narrow streets, the old buildings, and decided it would be good to leave. Which I ended up doing. My interviewer that day was perceptive, and advised me that I might find a more suitable job elsewhere.

I never would have thought that I'd have as much trouble finding a job in America as I did. It seemed that there were many jobs advertised all over the place, but I received just as many types of excuses explaining why I was not eligible for each and every job I applied for. At one company, where I had passed both the aptitude and typing tests, I was told that they employed citizens of the United States only—I had a long way to go yet before becoming a U.S. citizen.

My husband and I were not even immigrants yet. Gamil had come from the United Kingdom on a visa called exchange visitor J1, and I was a J2, his spouse. This is a special visa they gave physicians who came to the United States if they weren't coming as immigrants. It enabled them to train, pay taxes, and to have their spouse stay in the country for a longer period of time than a normal visitor's visa allowed. But it did not permit the spouse to work in the States, at least not in every place. In order for me to work, I would have to have my status changed, or look for work at specific places.

With this knowledge in mind, I turned to the employment agencies. I believed they would know better where to find a job for someone in my situation. The employees at the agency, after giving me various tests, began the difficult task of placing me in a suitable position. They worked hard. One afternoon, I was waiting for a long time in the reception room while the agent was making phone contacts in the office. He apparently had lost hope of finding me a job, so he called me into his office to observe and witness his efforts. I sat down and listened to a one-way conversation that went something like this:

AGENT: "Mr.——, I have a young lady here at my office looking for a job. Her qualifications match your request."
EMPLOYER: "——————."
AGENT: "She's Egyptian, speaks pretty good English, and she passed our tests."

EMPLOYER: "————————."
AGENT: "She can understand me, and I speak pretty fast."
EMPLOYER: "————————."
AGENT: "Okay. Thanks."

The agent then hung up the phone, and with his right hand still on the receiver he turned his face (with a big mustache) toward me, his shaggy eyebrows raised, his eyes half closed as though in a squint, and the corners of his mouth turned down, drawing the big mustache down his chin. Finally he spoke up and said, "This is the way it has been every time." I was very discouraged; I wondered what exactly I should do.

"Thank you," I murmured, getting ready to leave.

He said quickly, "Wait a minute." He then made one last call and Personnel at that company made an appointment for me. The agent asked me to stop at the agency after my appointment, which I did.

I told him what happened when I had gone to Binney & Smith, the Crayola crayon makers. Personnel informed me, after interviewing me, that the person I would work for, Mrs. Donne, was out sick. Since she would be my boss, it was necessary for her to interview me when she came back to work. Was this another put-off?

The agent's face showed his skepticism. He was positive it was just another excuse not to employ me, and he made no effort to hide his thoughts. He went right to the phone and began his search again, advising me, in the meantime, to keep my appointment with this Mrs. Donne at Binney & Smith. It was set for the next day.

When I finally met Mrs. Donne, I just could not make up my mind about her. I did not dislike her, but I wondered what she would be like to work for. Her voice was deep and her personality was overpowering. She said she liked my background, which surprised me as well as gave my spirits a big lift. After all the rejections, it was wonderful to hear! She was the only employer so far who had liked me—and she was hiring me for it!

As time went on, I learned that people with college degrees did not usually apply for such jobs, as those with a high-school diploma could handle them. But they did hire me, so I had to make some changes in my schedule.

I went back to the business school and asked to switch classes from the day session to the evening one. When my teacher, Mrs. Smith, heard the reason, she was unpleasantly surprised that I'd gotten a job.

I had been paying the school ten dollars for every extra week that I had to stay over the "guaranteed" eight weeks. Mrs. Smith would examine each and every one of my papers as if under a microscope, looking for errors that were erased and corrected, and then she would call me to show me how I did not do the job of erasing well enough because the error was still showing. One particular error she referred to was on the copy, not on the letter, and we had been told that we didn't even have to correct the copy. I could see the other teacher with the corner of my eye, sitting next to Mrs. Smith, shaking her head in disbelief at her criticism.

It was Mrs. Smith's perfectionism that had prompted me to look for a job and move on with my life. I was so glad to switch to the evening class, as I was ready to pass my 120-words-per-minute test and graduate.

The screening test in the evening classes was given every meeting. The first session I attended I took the test and passed. According to the regulations of the school, a student who passed the final test had to bring the test paper to the school office for them to issue the certificate. I took my exam paper after it was corrected and went to the office to turn it in and receive my certificate. But as I stepped into the office, Mrs. Smith was having a chat with the secretary, who was a good friend of hers. I walked in with a smile, but Mrs. Smith's face turned pale and long. She gasped, "You passed?" Joyfully I said, "Yes I did!" —not realizing that she was upset about my passing. She said to leave the paper with the secretary and that the test paper and certificate would be mailed to me as soon as the necessary work was completed. I waited for days, weeks, and months, but no certificate arrived in the mail.

I called the school secretary. Politely she apologized about the delay, and then added that the certificate was right there in her drawer. "All I have to do is stamp it and mail it to you. I am so sorry for the inconvenience." I believed her and continued to wait. Although I called several times thereafter, her answer was always the same.

Finally I decided to stop at the school during my lunch hour and pick up the certificate myself. *After all,* I thought, *Forty-second Street and Avenue of the Americas*—where the school was—*is not that far from Madison Avenue and Forty-seventh Street.* So I walked down to the school, got on the elevator, and went up to the third floor. The doors of the elevator opened and I was faced with the secretary, who was waiting to go downstairs. Her face turned red and angry. In a defensive tone she said, "It's my lunch hour." I calmly stated that it should not take too long to hand me the certificate that was in her drawer. She pointed to the manager's office and said, "Report me," as she stepped into the elevator. I thought to myself, *That's exactly what I'll do.*

I walked into the manager's office. He was getting ready to leave for lunch as well. He tried to tell me that everything would be okay, but I didn't listen because by this time I was very angry. I said to him, trying hard to remember to control my temper, "Will you please listen to me?" He pulled a cigarette from the pack on his desk, not saying a word (that was 1970 and everyone smoked freely, anytime and anywhere), sat down at his desk, and listened to me. I told the story from day one at school, till that last incident by the elevator. Then I let him know that the story was complete and I would like an answer and my certificate.

He asked me for my full name, began checking some papers in his drawer, then left the room for another office. I did not know what he was doing. I was rather disturbed by then. Had I allowed myself to do what I felt like doing by this time, I would have left.

He came back to the door with a bunch of papers in his hand and asked me to follow him, this time to the superintendent's office. The manager left and I was asked to take a seat. The office was big and nicely furnished, not with metal desks like the rest of the school offices, but with real wood furniture, a cushioned sofa, and chairs. My mental concentration was directed toward controlling my nerves, trying to calm down and not overreact in anger.

The superintendent asked me what the problem was. I again explained that I had passed all my tests, had paid all the fees plus the extra per-week cost because it had taken me longer to complete the course, and that the secretary just would not give me my certificate even though I had come in person to receive it rather than have her go through the trouble of mailing it. I found this an opportunity to point out her behavior when she'd met me at the elevator. I told him that I was going back to work, but I would like to get my certificate. I said that all the information I gave him should have been enough to satisfy the school requirements. He said that he had no idea why the certificate was not mailed to me and that he would look into the matter that afternoon. If there was a problem, he would call me. Otherwise I should stop after work and pick it up. I left his office feeling a little better.

I completed my day at Binney & Smith without hearing from him. One of the secretaries at the office knew my story and wanted to go with me to the school, because she felt that I was not fighting hard enough for my rights. I thanked her and told her that if they didn't give me my certificate that evening then I would ask her to go with me when I went back. Her parents were first-generation immigrants and she understood the vulnerability foreigners felt while on strange ground, and how standing up for one's self can be like trying to hold up your body when your feet are injured. I appreciated her interest in my case but did not really want to take someone to speak for me.

This time the secretary was at her desk. When she saw me, she pulled the envelope containing my certificate and final exam paper out of her drawer and threw it at arm's length in my direction. It slid over her desk and, before I could catch it, it went flying into the corner of the room. While I was trying to rescue the envelope, she was saying, "Here. Get away with it!" When I heard this, I became both hurt and angry. Did I have to collect my certificate from the very floor? My eyes filled up with tears, and with my voice choking I said, "I paid more than any other student for this certificate. I earned it, I'm not getting away with anything."

I picked up the envelope and headed toward the hall, but unlike my usual self, I was unable to control my feelings. I was talking audibly, saying, "Is this where people come to learn good business manners? Collecting a certificate from the floor is not the normal way to receive a certificate. What did I do—other than be born in a different country—to deserve this treatment?" When I ran out of English words, I turned to Arabic to express more strongly how I felt. That made heads peek out of offices all around! I was afraid they'd call the police, so I turned toward the staircase rather than wait for the elevator. I ran down the stairs, assuring myself that I would never ever enter that building again as long as I lived.

I headed home, but going to that apartment in Brooklyn was not exactly "home, sweet home."

2
My First Two Years in the USA

Our apartment on Ashland Avenue was leased by the Brooklyn-Cumberland Medical Center, where Gamil was to do his residency. He had graduated from Cairo University Medical School and left Egypt for the United Kingdom, where he continued his medical education. He trained in Ireland, Scotland, Wales, and England for eight years, then decided to leave the United Kingdom for the United States. He took the necessary examinations to do his residency in America.

In 1968, he left the United Kingdom to start his residency training at Lincoln Medical Center, Bronx, New York. While on vacation in Egypt in the spring of 1969, we were engaged. He then returned to the Bronx. In the summer of 1969 he went back to Egypt for the wedding, after arranging for his second year of residency in Brooklyn, New York. We left Egypt for Brooklyn, a few days after the wedding. We had to live close to the medical center because of Gamil's frequent duties. This neighborhood was not an area where one would choose to live. Not all our apartment building was leased to hospital staff, only a few were. We were surrounded by drug addicts and purse snatchers.

Muggings occurred daily. Fights at every street corner were common. It was a frightful experience.

In Egypt we didn't have this kind of poverty. There were panhandlers who were in need of food for their families, and there were pickpockets who relieved people of their wallets without physically harming them. But poverty there seemed to me to be a social phenomenon, a result of a lack of education or job opportunity, where as here it struck me as more violent, and a choice despite opportunity.

Our Brooklyn neighborhood would have been tolerable, however, had the condition of the apartment been a bit better than what it was. I considered it to be a curse.

Mice and roaches invaded the whole building. We waged war on our unwanted guests to get rid of them. I had to let my family in Egypt know what my apartment in America was like, so I wrote my sister a letter:

September 10, 1969

Dear Samia,

<u>There are roaches and mice in America!</u> They are right here in our apartment and I am in shock, as you can probably tell.

You know, I never had to deal with any such thing in Egypt. Our home was always spotless and Mother unforgiving when it came to the question of cleanliness. Housemaids were never able to put up with her required standards. Professional cleaners were never satisfactory in her judgment.

I cannot tolerate the sight of roaches. As for mice, when they run as fast as they do, I lose my calm.

Last night, we came home after a very pleasant evening in Manhattan, where we had dinner and attended a Broadway show. We opened the door of the apartment and a mouse took off, running down the hallway from the living room to the bathroom; Gamil took off after it! I was so disturbed, I can't even remember what the play was about. All my pleasant memories were wiped out.

I cannot believe I am living in America!

I will keep writing to update you with the latest news.

Love to you and all your family,
Mary

We experimented with every roach and insect killer we could find on the market, but it was all in vain until one day, while shopping at Macy's, we found the ideal solution. We had gone to the housewares department, and our eyes fell upon a can containing powder called Nev-a-Mo. An orange-and-white label made the can very distinct, and the contents turned out to be amazing in their power.

We sprinkled the floor and corners of each room, and the roaches died instantly by the dozen. We got the apartment clean of roaches!

As for the mice, we had to consult with the superintendent of our building. He said that there were rather large openings around the heating ducts and mice traveled through them, going from one apartment to the next. He suggested plaster to block the openings, and eventually we made the place mouseproof.

One day our next-door neighbor, a musician, noticed that I was sprinkling white powder on the threshold to our apartment. He asked me what it was, and I told him that it was to kill the roaches before they came inside the apartment. He asked for the name of the powder. I was glad to show him the can of Nev-a-Mo and tell him where to get it so that he too could rid his apartment of the pests.

During the time we lived in Brooklyn, I either went to the business school Monday through Friday, or went to work at Binney & Smith. Toward the end of two years, I left the Crayola makers and worked for a temporary agency, doing various office jobs at different businesses.

My husband was on call every other weekend, and I found those weekends most difficult and boring. He would leave on Saturday morning, and I would try to keep myself busy working around the apartment. I did not want to go out because I was too scared by all the horror stories I heard about street crime. Saturdays went by fairly easily, but Sundays never did. I did not enjoy TV—we had no cable then, no movie videos, just the three or four main channels—and that was all the entertainment we had. Reading literature was no fun then, because I was so restless. Looking at the five locks on the door gave me the feeling of being in a prison, which added to my unhappiness. Some Sunday evenings I struggled really hard, trying to stop myself from smashing my head against the wall to get rid of my misery. I never did anything crazy to myself, though.

On weekends when Gamil was not on call, we would go shopping and run our errands on Saturday mornings, then in the evening we would go to Manhattan for a walk, dinner, or a show. What I enjoyed most was Radio City Music Hall. The Rockettes were spectacular, giving a breathtaking professional performance in good taste. Madison Square Garden and Lincoln Center were amazingly huge buildings. They held large numbers of audiences and provided good entertainment such as the Ice Capades and Holiday on Ice. Fifth Avenue, Park Avenue, Rockefeller Plaza—here was the America I had expected to find.

One Saturday we stood in line for two and a half hours to get tickets for a show at Radio City. The line surrounded the whole block, and that long wait introduced me to pretzels. The little cart with its stock of twisted, hot breadsticks reminded me of a similar-looking snack we used to eat at the movies in Egypt. Called *semeet*, it was a circle of soft bread with sesame seeds on it.

Broadway's lights and advertisements were dazzling and impressive. And I loved our walks. Down Broadway to Times Square we'd go, and over to Fifth Avenue with all its famous stores, with their beautiful windows offering the latest in world fashions. Their unique items made window-shopping a great pleasure.

Once we got to Rockefeller Plaza we would walk the pretty path, then go down the few steps to the lower plaza to see the huge golden statue, watch the ice skaters enjoy their sport, and listen to the music playing from speakers—soft classical music or, if it was December, music fitting to the season. The atmosphere was soothing, it took me and all my senses away from the tension of the buzzing city. During the summer months, the ice rink became an open-air garden-style restaurant, with cheerfully colored umbrellas and tables. Eating there felt like sitting by the seaside and being served a complete meal of fresh green salad, lightly baked chicken, and sautéed vegetables while relaxing.

Sometimes, on Saturday evenings, we would ride the bus from Manhattan, through the Upper West Side, all the way up to the higher-numbered streets of Harlem, a part of America we hadn't known existed. Gamil and I both loved to discover through travel, and in that year we were trying to understand the city of New York, so we went on these evening rides on near-empty buses to satisfy our curiosity. We found that there were places in New York even worse than where we lived in Brooklyn.

Some of the areas we saw were nice, yet so many others were old and run-down that when we'd return to Brooklyn I would wonder, *Are we doomed to live in a place like this forever? Not destined to live in anything like the homes near Central Park or the one we went to, in the lovely suburbs, to attend a party given by the head of Gamil's department?*

That home was the site of our first Christmas party in New York. We were given a ride, since we didn't have a car. The house was spacious and pretty, warm and cozy. But as we were leaving to go home, I began to wonder how someone might have spilled a big bag of flour all over the lawn, for it was covered with something white. As I was thinking this, Gamil's friend who was driving us said, "Oh, the snow's covered the ground already!"

This was my first winter and my first encounter with snow. I asked friends to teach me how to walk in it, with short steps and with heels first—after I had fallen a couple of times! I also found out that high boots are a necessity in New York in winter, not a luxury.

That first winter, I had an ear infection and I went to see a specialist. The nurse called my name and I did not respond. It might have been partly because of the severity of the ear infection, but she was calling me by my married name, Mary Khair, and I was not used to that yet. Women in Egypt do not change their maiden name, it is one's identity from birth till death. There, I would be addressed as Mrs. Gamil Khair, using the full name of my husband or if using my first name, it would be followed by my maiden name, and I would be called Mary Rizk. The nurse was also pronouncing Gamil's last name incorrectly, as was usually the case. I'd heard it pronounced *Chair, Hair,* and *Ka-hair,* but that day I just could not figure out what she was saying. Finally she held the paper with my name up to my face and asked me if that was my name. Then I knew she was calling on me!

The summer of 1970 was my first summer in the States. My mother and my sister Samia, with her family, came to visit me. It made me feel really good that they were taking the time, effort, and expense to come all the way from Egypt. I would have loved to receive them in a spacious, nicer, and more comfortable home. But our furniture was still old and worn, the weather was hot and humid, and the air-conditioning units were too loud for us to enjoy a peaceful conversation. Worse yet, I had started that hard-won full-time job at Binney & Smith less than a month before they arrived, so I had no accrued vacation time in which to take them sightseeing. All in all, my guests were inconvenienced and I felt quite badly about it because I was unable to offer them the best, as my Egyptian tradition and upbringing taught me.

Living in Brooklyn taught me a lot. I learned about muggings, purse snatchings, robberies at gunpoint, and killings in apartments. Though, in Egypt, pickpockets were something I had had to watch out for as I was growing up, in Brooklyn I felt surrounded by the constant threat of crime.

Several incidents happened to people who worked at the hospital and lived in the building where we did. A doctor who was walking from one hospital to the other was stopped and relieved of his wallet and watch at knifepoint. A couple at the grocery store, ahead of us in the cashier's line, left to go home, taking the same route we would. They were stopped by a group of young men who quickly took their wallets at gunpoint. Fortunately for us, by the time we left the store the robbers were gone. Unfortunately for the couple, we saw no sign of their being accosted, so we couldn't help them. We didn't know about it until the next day, when they told Gamil at work. We were both sad for them, and glad they were not hurt.

One afternoon, while I was in the laundry room in the basement waiting for a load of wash, I was reading the notices on the bulletin board. The first one I read was as follows: $500.00 REWARD FOR ANYONE WHO GIVES THE POLICE A LEAD TO THE KILLER OF MR. JONES IN APARTMENT 14J. It hit my brain like lightning. A killer was one floor away from us. I never went back to the laundry room alone.

"The City of Contrasts" was what I called New York. The pretty suburban homes and our apartment in Brooklyn; Fifth

Avenue and Harlem; Broadway shows and my lonely weekends; the muggings, the killings, and robberies caused by poverty and the rich life lived by the Rockefellers and others. All this provided for confusion and inability to decide whether I liked or hated New York.

At school and at work, I learned to observe people and their different attitudes, the variety of their lifestyles and their ways of behaving. As an example, I noticed what I later called "the American singularity of topic." When two or more Americans talk, they start a subject, say sports, they keep that topic going on for the balance of the visit. One may leave and come back, only to find the subject still the same after hours of discussion. It is not even unusual if the next day, over lunch, the same people are still discussing the same topic from the day before. This is not just my observation. It was observed by an Egyptian friend at his place of business too. By contrast, Egyptians enjoy what I call a plurality of topics. A host there would be considered lacking hospitality if the topic of conversation did not change every now and then.

Another interesting observation is that some adults study different religions and then they become involved, by choice, in one of the religions, after studying and deciding that it is the religion he or she wants to follow. Egypt has two main religions: Christianity and Islam. The child born to a family of one religion or the other grows up to be a member of that religion. Changing religion is not an option.

Not all my observations were so serious, though. One funny experience occurred one day after school as I was walking with my friend toward the subway station. Some young people were there handing out flyers. I took one, not knowing what it was about. My friend started laughing and said, "Why are you taking that? You don't need it, you're already married." I asked her, "What is it about?" She said it was an advertisement for computer dating. I laughed. "A modern-day matchmaker!"

As our two years in New York were approaching an end, the question arose as to whether Gamil should spend another year at Brooklyn-Cumberland Medical Center as a resident in general medicine or look into going to a different medical facility to become a specialist. There was no hesitation on my part; I did not want to live in Brooklyn for yet another year. If he chose to stay there, I said, I was going to go to Egypt for that year and come back after he had moved out of New York. I knew by then that New York City did not properly represent the United States. In fact, I was told by more than one American, if we wanted to know the country, we should leave New York and live in other states.

Once the decision was made that we would leave New York, the search began. Gamil sent out applications for a fellowship in cardiology in the neighboring states, since that was the field he decided to make his speciality in. At the same time I had had enough of working for Mrs. Donne at Binney & Smith. She had a terribly loud voice, and I did not like that. My friend at the office, also named Mary, was my only consolation there, other than the paycheck.

The trips to and from work were unforgettable! The subway trains in the morning were packed like cans of sardines. People were impatient; they stepped on each others' feet, and the result was always an unpleasant reaction. Some would vent angry words that I couldn't find in the dictionary at the end of the day; others would respond to the expression "sorry" with, "I didn't die." That always left me wondering, *When do you apologize and when don't you in New York?* I left with this question unanswered.

One morning, while the subway train was between two stations, the electricity went out and the train stopped. It was scary. Being underground in the dark, with no movement, I pictured the train as a coffin and thought, *This must be how death feels!* I considered myself dead, and hoped that hell would be a better place than Brooklyn. After about forty-five minutes, the electricity was restored and the train started to move. I got off at the first stop and called the office to explain my tardiness. A very angry Mrs. Donne answered. I told her that as soon as I knew where I was and found the transportation—above ground—to bring me to the office, I would be there.

Another frightening incident on the subway happened to me one day after work. The weather was hot and very humid. I had to wait for the subway for a very long time. Both the station and the train were packed, due to the delay in trains. Just before my train arrived at my stop, I fainted and fell to the floor of the train. The passengers were worried; they tried to shake me back to life but I was totally unconscious and they got no response from me.

Then I started to revive and I opened my eyes. I saw one passenger reaching for the red rope that ran along the sides of the train, above the windows, to alert the train's engineer that there was a dangerous situation on the train. When he saw I was awake he stopped, and said to me, "I thought you were dead."

When the plan was final that we would be moving to Hartford, Connecticut, I decided to resign my job at Binney & Smith and spend time getting ready to move. I found myself being congratulated by other secretaries the day I submitted my resignation. They told me that I was the secretary who had worked for Mrs. Donne the longest time without quitting—and that was only for six months. The one before me had worked for one week, and the one before her had only stayed for half a day—during her lunch hour she typed a note and left it in the typewriter, telling Mrs. Donne that she was impossible to work for, therefore she was not returning after lunch. In another department, the manager asked his secretary, "Why is it that secretaries don't stay long with Mrs. Donne?" I realized then that I had a good reason to be unhappy during the six months I worked at Binney & Smith, and was justified in deciding to leave earlier than was absolutely necessary.

Since it was a few months yet before we had to move to Hartford, I went to a temporary employment agency so that I could work when I had the time, and attend to moving arrangements as needed.

This choice was good for more than one reason: not only did it facilitate my time management, but I learned, in a short time, about a variety of businesses and different types of people. I was tested by the agent and started my assignments according to the days of my choice. Some assignments were as short as one day; others as long as I wanted to stay. Some places were gloomy; others were cheerful. Some people liked my presence, since I was there to help; others resented it and couldn't hide their displeasure. All in all, it was a learning experience for me.

I also found out that some places, when they asked for temporary help, described the job for the agency one way, but when the temporary help arrived at the office she would find that the work required was much more than had been described. The reason for this was that they didn't want to pay the employment agency the higher fee for the more involved work. I was told by the agency that, in cases such as this, I should call the agency right away and explain the situation.

Among the places that I enjoyed working was a company located on the third floor of the Empire State Building. The location made it interesting. When I arrived that first morning, I asked at the information desk for directions to the company where I was going to work. They sounded simple enough. When I got to the third floor, though, there were halls up and down, right and left, and offices everywhere. Each floor seemed to be a little city of its own, with its streets and intersections. Using a public phone in one of the hallways, I stopped and called the agency for help in finding the office. I told them that I'd gotten to the building, and to the third floor, but that I was lost somewhere on that floor! I was asked to give them the phone number where I was calling from and to hang up and wait for them to call me back after they'd checked the location with the secretary at my destination. They did that, and I found the office. When I arrived at the door I was greeted by the employees with a welcome suitable for someone lost, then found, in space—not just down the hallway!

I spent three pleasant days on that job. Once I completed it, I was asked to go to another company for two days. When I got there, I was dictated an enormous letter of more than ten pages. The boss was obviously under a lot of tension and very nervous, which made the atmosphere very uncomfortable to work in. At the end of the first day, I was ready to leave, with the intention of calling the agency to let them know that I was not willing to return the next day to complete this assignment. My boss, though, told me to consider the job complete and not to come back the next day. Our feelings were mutual; neither one of us was comfortable with the other.

Many of my temp jobs were in typing pools, where I felt as if I'd joined a herd of cattle. These seemed very dehumanizing to me.

My best assignment in New York City was the one where I also stayed the longest, and left only because I had to attend to the preparation for the move. That company was a clothing company that imported women's apparel from Taiwan and sold it to New York retail stores. It was located in New York's garment district, just a few blocks from Macy's department store. Loads of dresses and garments were being hauled on racks through the streets, wheeled by men at all times of the day. This was a common sight, very characteristic of this area.

The setup of the company's office was open: a huge hall, desks lined up and down, little fitting rooms on either side of the hall. The group of employees was a happy one: they talked, joked, worked, and helped one another. But when the information about the arrival time of ships and a shipment's contents started to come from overseas over the telex machine, the place was quiet except for the sound of the machine delivering the message. This meant that the young man in charge had to concentrate, and a lot of work followed for everyone.

My part of the job was mainly typing tables, which called for some precise work, as well as some other paperwork. Because I liked the place, I enjoyed the work and surprised them by doing a good job. They asked me about my nationality. That was the time when Nasser was president of Egypt, and that provided for a rich topic of jokes. I laughed along but never had any input to offer.

The most entertaining assignment, though, was a one-day job. It was at another company that imported goods from the Far East. When I arrived, the boss met me and asked me to sit down at the secretary's desk. He went on to explain to me that his secretary was very efficient, busy, her work was very confusing, and she took excellent care of everything. She was absent, he said, because she had to attend a funeral. And it was an especially important day at the office, because their supplier from the Far East was paying a visit. I was then told not to touch anything on the desk, as this might mix up the secretary's work, and I was to "look very busy!"

I was silent for a second, trying to absorb what he had said. I think he then realized that what he was asking for was very unusual. He turned around and quickly left, walking toward his office. I was upset by this situation; I liked to work, not to make believe. To be used as a dummy at the desk did not appeal to me. I did not want to call the agency to report the type of work asked of me. It took me a few minutes to calm my thoughts, and to convince myself that I was getting a day's pay for doing nothing. It would be good enough to sit down and act busy without touching anything on the desk! All this thinking took just a brief moment or two, and I started playing secretary. The day passed uneventfully.

The month of June was approaching, and it was at the end of June that we had to leave New York for Hartford, Connecticut. The apartment in which we were to live in Hartford was made available by St. Francis Hospital, where my husband was going for his fellowship training in cardiology. The apartment was not furnished, so we had to do some shopping in Hartford. This was our second trip to that city.

The first one had been in November, when we had both had a day off. Knowing that we were going to move the following June, we decided to spend it getting acquainted with the new city. We went on the Greyhound bus on that day, the fourth Thursday of the month.

Hartford was smaller than New York, and much cleaner. When we got hungry, late that afternoon, we went to a restaurant and waited to be seated. A worn-out waitress came up to us and said, "I can seat you, but don't ask for turkey, because we are out of turkey." Neither of us was a turkey lover, and we never ordered turkey when we ate out. We wondered why she would assume that we would order turkey? We were rather offended by the unfriendly greeting, but nevertheless chose to stay and be seated with the unsolved mystery in our minds about why we might have ordered turkey, according to the waitress.

A year later, while in Hartford, I learned about Thanksgiving. Then I understood why the fourth Thursday in November had been a day off and why the restaurant was out of turkey by the time we got there! Later, when we had children in school, we began to participate in the "turkey day" celebration.

The experience at the restaurant in Hartford symbolized the difficulties in communication that occur when two cultures meet. We were two people speaking the same language, physically close, standing a couple of feet from each other, and even though we were talking about food, we were continents, oceans, and cultures apart. Trying hard to grasp and understand seemed like trying to hug the horizon: Sometimes it seemed as if one almost understood the other culture, only to find that what had been thought to be understanding was actually a mirage. Sometimes the effort to blend two cultures ends up separating them, as water does from oil.

Trying to achieve homogeneity between cultures should not be the ultimate goal, I believe. Rather, there should be a patient, tireless interest in understanding and in accepting each one as he or she is. This approach would bring happiness and peace.

On our second visit to Hartford shortly before the actual move, we went once again to check the apartment and buy the furniture needed for it. The hospital had a good arrangement: The doctors who had families were provided with two-story houses, located across the street from the hospital. Single doctors, or those married but with no children, were provided an apartment in the brand-new four-story building the hospital had built for them. The fact that the building was new was a special treat for me after the worn-out Brooklyn apartment building we were coming from. They gave us a list of strict rules and regulations, but the new refrigerator and stove made up for them.

Once we knew the size of our apartment, we went to look for furniture. It seemed that we had a lot of time, so we prepared a long list of furniture store addresses. We checked our map and started with the one that was the farthest away. Our intention was to visit them all, and end with the one closest to downtown, where we could catch the bus back to New York. It was not as wise a plan as it seemed. By the time we arrived at the farthest one, our time had been used up by traveling. The place looked shabby and old. The furniture there reflected the appearance of the building. We were in a predicament and had no outlet, no time to visit Hartford again before we moved.

The very old salesman, Mr. Morris, sensed our at-a-loss condition and asked us to sit down by him on one of the sofas. Like a respectable father, he started talking us into seeing the furniture as ideal and reasonable for our purpose and purse. Mr. Morris's effect on us was stronger than any sedative for our taste in furniture. We ended up buying all we needed. A living room set, a bedroom set, and a dining room set. We left to return to New York, unsure of what we had done but soothed by the fact that the adviser was a mature man who could not be wrong.

When the day to move came we rented a U-Haul trailer, and our friends came over from Queens to hook the trailer to their car and help us move. We loaded the trailer with our personal belongings, thinking we didn't have that much to move. To our surprise, we had a very hard time trying to fit everything on the trailer. We were already tired by the time we finished putting everything on, and now we were facing a long drive of 150 miles or more to Hartford to unload, then return to New York.

It was hectic with six people in the car, which included our friends' two children. When we arrived in Hartford, we unloaded the U-Haul. The new furniture wasn't due to be delivered yet, since we were returning to New York for a few more days. We had to sit on the floor and rest a little bit before starting the return trip. I couldn't help but remember when my family had moved from one apartment to another in Cairo, in 1965. The movers arrived, our cousins and neighbors gave us a helping hand, the furniture was loaded, and the distance was short; at the other end, cousins and friends helped put everything in place and in a few hours we were ready to start life in the new apartment. I missed that comparatively easy life I'd had in Egypt.

That summer (1971), we went to visit our relatives in Egypt before starting work in Hartford. It was our first trip home since coming to the States as newlyweds in September of 1969. Everyone at home was anxious to see us and listen to what we had to say, to learn about our experience firsthand rather than from letters. We were just as eager to share with them what they wanted to hear.

We enjoyed warm welcomes, generous meals, and lots of the kind of attention I had missed all along, especially during our move to Hartford. We traveled from Cairo to Alexandria to see as many members of both families as we possibly could.

This much-needed visit rejuvenated us, giving us that energy that comes only from a sense of belonging. Though both Gamil and I had made changes to adjust to surroundings and circumstances, I saw now that the original person within each of us was unchanged, just waiting for a catalyst to emerge:

>CATALYST
>
>In the sandy Sahara Desert,
>I was born.
>Next to Cheops.
>On the Sphinx's lap, I took my nap.

Ramses' great-granddaughter,
My classmate.
Cleopatra, not a wrinkle,
Taught me lessons in skin care,
Watercress her secret.

Uprooted, fly away; in the arms
Of opportunity I landed.
Dug fresh roots, right here
In the melting pot,
Catalyst I am.

When we returned to Hartford from our vacation in Egypt, we had to readjust to being in the United States once again. And to being in Hartford after living in New York City. It was a change in our pace of living not unlike the change of seasons.

3
Moving to New England

There was no subway system in Hartford and that was good news for me. I had suffered from the overcrowded morning trains, sometimes even getting stuck and frightened in their dark and damp tunnels, for two years. But there was no Broadway, Radio City Music Hall, Fifth Avenue, or Rockefeller Center either.

My husband's schedule was much better in Hartford. When he was on call, he had to be available but he didn't necessarily have to stay day and night at the hospital, as was the case in Brooklyn. I didn't have to experience long boring weekends anymore. Also, our whole apartment building was occupied by the medical staff of St. Francis Hospital so, unlike the apartment building in Brooklyn, this one had a family atmosphere. Even doing laundry became easier; we had a laundry room on every floor. No more going downstairs to the basement, and because it was safe, I could go alone.

We were able to find our way around Hartford and West Hartford easily. We bought our first car, an off-white Renault.

I took driving lessons, but my lessons were taught on an automatic car and the Renault was standard transmission. I had to go through some extra training to drive our car. We were able to go to New York to visit old friends and to New Haven to visit new ones. We went to weddings and Christmas parties without needing a ride from friends; this was our first plunge into American luxury!

As we were having a walk one day at the park in Hartford, we met an Egyptian couple. We became very good friends. They lived a few blocks away from us. During the two years we were in Hartford, we went out together almost every weekend, sometimes to dinner and movies, but most of all we enjoyed some magnificent New England drives that fall. We would pick them up early Saturday morning. Gamil would have mapped a long driving route for us to feast our eyes on. We visited Plymouth, Massachusetts, to see where earlier immigrants had set foot; Vermont; New Hampshire; Maine; the Hudson River, above New York City; Bear Mountain State Park, in New York State, and Cape Cod. Sometimes we spent a weekend, sometimes just a full day. Nature outdoes itself in New England in the fall. My memories of the foliage are outstanding.

OCTOBER IN NEW ENGLAND

Van Gogh, Monet, Michelangelo,
Along with some others,
Gathered together
To view the fall.
The rolling hills bursting with color,
The mountains and the valleys
Dressed in nature's richest attire.
The miles of winding roads
Bending over with their loads
Of golden leaves aglitter,
Of purple, burgundy, orange,
And hues yet unnamed.
Their eyes unable to canvass this beauty,
They signed a declaration:
"Discard our art,
Let us depart,
We'll leave it to creation."

We were lured, not only by the beauty of nature, but also by civilization: by the paved country roads, the gas stations, inns, and restaurants along the way, the easy access to telephones, regardless of how remote the area was.

The city of Hartford and its downtown area were compact in comparison to New York City. We had Main Street in the center of the city, with all the major department stores, and Constitution Plaza, not too far from Main Street. This plaza was a center of attraction, especially during the holiday season. It was built like a bridge over the main Interstate. Pedestrians had to climb a few steps to get to the top, where the stores and banks were, as well as to the building that gave the plaza its own characteristic: a semicircular, all-glass, very high and modern building, housing Hartford Insurance. Constitution Plaza was cheerful, inviting a stroll because it was open and peaceful, since there were no cars or traffic lights. At Christmastime it was all aglow with lights and window decorations, which outdid all the decorations I'd seen even in Manhattan during the two previous years.

Going to graduate school was still on my mind, so I inquired about how to enroll at the University of Connecticut for courses leading to my master's degree in English literature. I was directed toward a series of courses related to working in a library. Though this was for professional certification only, and not for my master's, I gave that some thought and decided it might be the thing for me, so I applied. The courses were taught at one of the University of Connecticut's branches, which happened to be down the road from where we lived. The instructor, a library consultant, an eloquent, confident, middle-aged woman, made sure we knew at the first meeting that she was the wife of the medical professor of pathology at Yale Medical School. Mrs. Bernice Yesner was her name. She taught her courses twice a year, during the fall and spring. Sometimes she would teach a course in the summer, but that would take place at her home by the pool. Students who completed all five courses were qualified to receive the School Media-Aide Major Certificate.

Most of her students were either volunteer mothers at their children's schools who wanted to improve their general knowledge of how a library works, or professional librarians who wanted to update their knowledge. Every season that Mrs. Yesner taught a course while I was in Hartford, I was there to attend, until I completed all five. I enjoyed the courses, some more than others, and my degree of enjoyment showed in my work. I learned a lot about mending books; a skill I still use today. Storytelling for children was my strongest area. Even though I had to tell my stories to adults (the class), I was able to pretend that I was talking to children, and this helped my presentations. They were well received by the instructor.

Card cataloguing was my least interesting course. I never did get the cards in where they belonged. Later, when I worked for the Hartford Public Library, this continued to be the case, and I asked not to work in the card catalog department where I would have had to file cards, so I chose to work in mending and circulation. When library classes were not in session, I worked for a temporary agency. Once again, it was a good choice for me. It helped me know Hartford better and it gave me time off for the library courses or for traveling with my husband. Besides our weekend trips throughout New England, I had the opportunity during those two years to go to Chicago and to Dallas.

Hartford, I felt, had more to offer that I liked than what I disliked. I worked for three days at Heublein, Inc., in Farmington. The work there was monotonous. The secretary had let the boring work pile up until it was time for their inventory, then she asked her boss to hire temporary help to be able to catch up, which he did. To this day, every time I go to the store and see A.1. steak sauce, I'm reminded of that place. The work at the office was not as tasty as their goods.

Once that assignment was completed, I was asked to go to A. B. Dick in West Hartford, and I worked there for a number of weeks. That place gave me a chance to observe how servicemen were dispatched, how schedules and routes were planned for service calls, and to hear about some of their experiences on the job. I began to understand some of the situations they were faced with, for they often had to call the office for advice on how to repair a machine. There was a lot of gossip at A. B. Dick. I learned more about the temp agency I was working for, about the hiring and firing based on personal liking and disliking, than I would have ever heard at the agency itself.

I had a few other brief jobs; one was for a place that supplied computer materials. I never understood what I was typing. I had to fill in tables on the typewriter, but the whole thing didn't make any sense to me. I felt that I did not do a good job, but it was a one-day appointment anyway.

Then I was asked to go to a trucking company for a rather long assignment. The people there were very good to me, and the company was close enough to where I lived that I could walk to work when the weather permitted. The only unpleasant thing about that place was the strong odor of grease and oil that filled the whole building. They wanted me to stay week after week. I stayed as long as I could take it. Eventually, I had the opportunity to go to Dallas, and that was a good reason to terminate my assignment. They asked me to return to them after I was back from my trip, but I couldn't bring myself to do so.

In Dallas, life was very different from Hartford and that smelly company. I was impressed by the huge hotels, the fancy style shows, luncheons, dinners, city tours, and by shopping at major stores such as Neiman Marcus. Transportation was private, from the hotel to any location or tour. "Big D" left a big impression on me, there was no question about that! Its people were so determined to present their city as BIG as they possibly could. On one of the tours, a lady looked out the window and saw a grocery store displaying pumpkins. She turned to the tour guide and said, "Your pumpkins are the same size as the ones we have in our state." The guide, with a smile, answered, "But those are oranges, dear!" That prompted a good laugh from all the group on the bus.

After I returned from Dallas, I asked for another temporary job. This was the longest and also my last. It was for a collection agency. At first I didn't understand why I had to write out those mysterious cards. They said: *Please call 555-1234* (but the real phone number of the collection agency). An employee explained it to me. Upon receiving the card, a person would think he or she had won something and would call. At that point, one of the eloquent agents would speak to the caller, draw information about the individual's financial condition, and give advice on how to pay their outstanding bills.

On my way to work one morning, on the bus that crossed over from Hartford to West Hartford, an employee of the collection agency called out to me, saying, "If I were married to a doctor, I'd leave this job for someone who needed it." I was taken by surprise and didn't want to say anything that might aggravate the situation. When we arrived at the office, I did not mention the incident to anyone, but obviously she did. I was asked if I was upset by this woman's comment on the bus, and I was called for a meeting with the owner-manager of the company.

He told me that he should know about things that happen among employees that cause upset. He also said that people who do not work are lazy people who just want to sit down and do nothing, and that if he knew that he had one more day to live, he would spend it at work. Even with his kind words, it was an awkward situation and a very difficult day for me.

I was unable to settle down emotionally until after lunch. A good friend of mine from Egypt (not the one we frequently traveled with) worked for a different company in the same building. We often had pleasant lunches together. That day we talked about my morning and I felt better when I saw she understood my position: I was working in order to improve my understanding, both linguistically and culturally, of Americans. I was planning to stay home with my children when I had them, yet I wanted to know what it was like out there so I wouldn't have to learn about this new country through them.

The two years we were in Hartford were two very busy years, during which I learned more about living in the United States. My temporary work, which varied in length from one day to several weeks, made my paycheck different every week, but never did I expect a sixty-dollar check, which I received one day when I was supposed to receive a fifteen-dollar check only. I contacted the agency to tell them about my big check. They asked me to mail it back, which I did. They returned one for the correct amount and a very pleasant letter of gratitude.

That year I found out that a very important landmark was within walking distance from where we lived. It was Mark Twain's house. I had read this American author's novel, *The Adventures of Huckleberry Finn*, for my American literature course in college in Egypt. I had had the most difficult time trying to believe the characters and the adventures, to the point where I thought the author was not real. It was easier for me to picture Charles Dickens as a real person, writing about real-life misery, than to believe that Mark Twain could be writing about real-life experiences.

My sister Isis came to visit me from England, where she lived and practiced medicine, and we went together to tour Mark Twain's house. Also, my sister Samia, her son Moni and her daughter Mary Therese came to visit me and I took them to visit Mark Twain's as well. Each time I went, I listened hard to the stories the tour guide would tell us about the author, the owner of the house, and I would listen to his voice on the old telephone, on which there was a recording that seemed to bring Mr. Twain back to life. We also enjoyed the architecture of the house, which was built like a boat.

In the summer of 1972, Gamil and I planned on going on a tour of Europe. We wanted to see as many cities as we possibly could, so we joined an American Express tour to visit seven capitals in Europe. The countries on our itinerary were: England, Holland, Austria, Germany, Switzerland, France, and Italy. At the time, we were not American citizens yet, so we still had our Egyptian passports. That meant we had to apply for a visa to enter each and every one of the countries on the itinerary, a task for which I had to allow a lot of time and patience.

I had to take our passports and go to New York City, to apply for the visas at each consulate. I had to fill out their forms and submit our passports. Depending on each country's system, I would either have to leave the passports and return when they told me to do so, or I'd have to wait until they granted the visa. Some consulates were even willing to forward them to the next one for me. My first obstacle with this project was not any legal situation, rather it was New York City itself!

I had forgotten what lunchtime looked like in New York. I looked at my watch, and it was noon. The streets and avenues were packed with people; it was hard to believe that a year or so before I was one of those people at this hour. We do forget, or maybe we are never really aware of what we are in, until we look at it from the outside. That day the mob I found myself in looked to me as if a riot were likely to start rather than a large number of employees on their way to lunch.

I turned around and headed toward Forty-second Street, to Tad's Steak House. For a dollar and forty-nine cents, you got a

T-bone steak, grilled to your liking while you waited and watched the preparation. Then they added the garlic bread, baked potato, salad, and a soft drink. This was a treat for myself and a way to get back in the mood for New York City. I sat there eating my steak and comparing New York's buzz to Hartford's calm.

After lunch at Tad's and a review of my memories, I went back to tend to our visas. At the French consulate, the employee insisted on speaking in French, which gave me a bit of trouble since I had not practiced my French in about three years. I was finally able to express my request and was granted the visas. Then I went to the Italian consulate.

The first room I had to go to was packed solid with people, mostly students, and the air-conditioning unit was broken. Tempers were running short. I searched for the end of the line, then I joined it. After moving up very slowly for forty minutes, I was third in line from the desk. A young Italian man came up to me and frantically started yelling at me in Italian. He was pointing to himself and to the floor where I stood.

After he finished whatever he was saying, I said in English, "I didn't understand a word of what you just said." I was not trying to be funny, but the young man ahead of me in line bent down almost in half with laughter, and the once-again crowded room was filled with bursts of laughter and smiles. To this day, I don't know what he said, but I assume he was accusing me of taking his place in line, which was not the case.

I left the Italian consulate assuring myself that I would never again go to Italy as long as I needed a visa. But once I got to Italy, I changed my mind. I would go through anything to visit Italy again.

The day finally came when we were to start our trip. It was indeed worthwhile. The variety of people, cultures, and nature was beyond any imagination: from the maze of small canals and the waters of Venice to the Swiss Alps, from the diamond cutting in Amsterdam to the Eiffel Tower in Paris. The second we crossed a border, nature would change, as would the language and the currency. Each country was outstanding in its beauty and culture, in its history and art, in its different but equally warm hospitality. I could not miss out on an opportunity to express my feelings about travel:

TRAVEL

By air, by car,
By coach, by boat,
By rail, by cable.
Cruising the Danube,
Climbing the Alps,
Strolling down the Champs-Élysées.
Touring the Coliseum,
Visiting Pharaoh in his tomb,
Smiling back at Mona Lisa,
Staring at the royal jewelry,
Tossing pennies in the Trevi fountain,
Blinking at the twinkling of Amsterdam's diamonds
Canoeing the canals of Venice.
What a thrill!

Of all the cities we visited, Rome was the one that impressed me the most. That is because in Rome one can stand on almost any street in the city, look around, and see three different civilizations: the ruins of the ancient city presented in the wall that once surrounded it; the Renaissance statues and carvings decorating entrances of buildings; and the very modern streets such as Via Vennetto, where elegant coffeehouses line the street like those on the Champs-Élysées in Paris. I was impressed because Rome displays all three together, while in Cairo one has to leave the busy modern city and travel fifteen kilometers or more southwest to see the pyramids and the Sphinx, then go in a different direction to see old Cairo. Our tour of Europe was a huge success, and we enjoyed every single experience except for one.

That experience was having to get off the coach at every country's border to present our passports and have our visas checked before we were allowed entry along with everyone else on the bus. Needless to say, this raised the question among our traveling partners: "Why is it that Mary and Gamil have to get off the bus at every border?" We explained our passport situation and we thought that was the end of their questions.

But on our last evening in Rome, the whole group went to eat dinner at a lovely authentic restaurant. After dinner, one of the men on the tour, having enjoyed a generous amount of good Italian wine, stood up and came to our table, took us by the hand, and asked to be listened to by the group. He then started a political lecture saying, "If all Egyptians and Arabs were like these two, what problem would the Middle East have?" He went on and on. Never was I more self-conscious and uncomfortable than I felt at that time, and I just wanted the evening and the whole tour to come to an end as quickly as possible. But it didn't. And when I had recovered from this man's insensitive statement, I enjoyed the rest of our travels.

After our tour of Switzerland, the coach stopped just before the Swiss-German border for us to exchange some money before going into Germany. The tour guide always gave us an idea of approximately how much to exchange and of the rate on the same day. I went to exchange a little bit of money and walked out of the Swiss bank. Gamil took a look at my money and told me they'd given me more than they should have. Sarcastically I said, "How much, a penny more?" But my conscience bothered me. I looked behind me and saw that the tour guide, Mr. Guy Sneath, was coming. I told him what I'd paid at the bank and showed him what they'd given me back. He smiled and said, "They made an error but it is in your favor." I asked him if he would hold the bus until I fixed this matter and he was more than willing.

When I went to the same window and presented the money, the young man's face turned pale. He sank down into the chair behind him, looked at the man in the next window, and said something in German, then took back two-thirds of the money he had given me earlier. I left the bank for the bus, thinking to myself that I would not have been so surprised if this mistake had happened in any other country—but Switzerland, of all places!

After our grand tour of Europe, we returned to Hartford, and I applied for a part-time job at the Hartford Public Library. I was almost done with my library aide certification courses. While I was waiting to hear from the library's personnel office, I was also following the local news in Hartford. The transportation system was shutting down because of the bus drivers' strike, and Hartford was dreading a standstill. This was November of 1972, and the holiday season was approaching.

While Hartford was focused on this threat of disruption, I was struck by the fact that this entirely earthbound problem was making the city anxious in the same era that the country as a whole, and even much of the world, was thinking of, and beginning to, conquer outer space. It was only a few years before, in 1969, when the first manned spacecraft landed on the moon, and since then there had been much talk about more ambitious treks into space. I took it upon myself to inform my family halfway around the world that, while our astronauts had left gravity behind in an amazing vehicle of modern science and were walking in space, we on earth had no simple public transportation vehicle to take us to work. I wrote my mother a letter to update her on the situation in Hartford:

Dear Mother,

I know how you are always up-to-date with the international scene. There is no question in my mind that you are watching those satellites soaring, leaving gravity behind, totally dependent on guiding scientists' knowledge for being successful. You are constantly praying for them, as it is your habit, and for their families, and for their safe return to earth. Most probably, you are also using your famous expression, "I lived to see the day when (whatever is happening happens)."

What is not on the news, though, is the fact that right here in Hartford I am trying to get to work, but there is no means of transportation. I can't drive, because parking spaces are hardly available. So I get up very early in the morning and I start walking, all the way downtown. By the time I get there, my legs are in no shape to carry me for the rest of the day; then at the end of the day I start my hike back home, only to arrive close to bedtime.

I will write to you again soon,

Love,
Mary

The bus drivers' strike continued through March 1973. Traffic was choked with drivers who normally did not drive to work; the city was crippled. One morning, when I didn't have to go to work, my friend asked me to drive her to her place of business. She was employed at a store on Constitution Plaza, the center of the busy area. There was a wide multilane street that ran parallel to Constitution Plaza at a lower level where cars would drop off passengers, then join the traffic once again while the passenger, as a pedestrian, climbed the stairs to the plaza level. I drove her to work, and all four lanes were packed with cars. The police were organizing the traffic. It was common for a car to pull up to the curb, drop off a passenger, and join the traffic again. I did that too, and after I dropped her off, I tried to pull back to join the traffic, but the car stalled! I felt as if I was in a big vacuum: my ears, eyes, and all my senses went numb. When I got the car going, my delayed hearing ran this by me:

POLICEMAN, (in the loudspeaker): "Come on, lady, get this white car out of the way."

My senses awakened suddenly and I questioned myself: *"White car?" "Come on, lady?" "Out of the way?" This is directed to me!* Good thing I didn't hear it before I got the car going. I would have never been able to move had I heard him then!

The job at the Hartford Public Library covered a variety of skills. Part of the day, I spent mending books so that they could be returned to circulation. Later I typed a second set of the cards for the card catalog, a requirement of the fire insurance company. In the afternoon, I printed the titles on government pamphlets after they returned from binding. I had to treat the tape on the backing with certain liquids, let it dry, and using a paintbrush, I wrote the title in white. When the employee whose job was to put the jackets on the new hardback books was very ill and on sick leave for a month, I did her job. I ended up working with just about everyone in the library and in every department.

The only job I dreaded, so I asked not to do it, was filing the cards back in the card catalog drawers. I worked at the Hartford library for four months before I found out that we were to leave Hartford for Milwaukee.

The end of June 1973 was the end of the second year of Gamil's fellowship, and he was to start his full-time staff position at the Veterans' Administration Hospital in Milwaukee, Wisconsin. I resigned sadly, although I had a lot to look forward to—we were expecting our first child in November of that year.

I asked the head of the department not to "pass the box"— a box that was passed around every time an employee was leaving in order to collect money and buy a gift for that person.

I had heard other employees object to the box, and rightly so, I thought. I wanted people to treat me the way they felt, not to be under any pressure. She assured me that she would not pass the box, but that she would not be responsible for individuals who might want to express their own feelings. I told her this was just what I wanted.

As the time approached for me to leave, Penny, to whom I had given a couple of rides on my way home when I had the car, took me out to lunch one day. Lucy gave me a pretty handkerchief and told me how much she loved me and that her gift was a simple token of affection. She also said she couldn't afford a better gift, and that a handkerchief in her culture (Italian) was given to a friend who was leaving as a symbol of continued friendship. I assured her that her gift was of great value to me, which it was. What I didn't tell her, though, was that in *my* culture, when someone is moving a gift of handkerchiefs is the exact opposite. It symbolizes the wiping of tears and the ending of the friendship.

Frances, the lady I helped with book mending, gave me a hug and told me that she loved me. Elizabeth, who substituted when the manager was away and never thought I was qualified to do anything, gave me a firm handshake and a good luck wish. As for Diane, as always, she turned her face the other way every time I passed by her. She did the same thing the last day, too. Previously, she had only looked for situations to embarrass me with regard to my home country.

I was happy I got what I wanted from each one: their honest feelings toward me.

It was then time to learn about our new destination. I had never heard of Milwaukee before. *What if there are no people living there?* I thought to myself. But then I would hear the answer from within: *They wouldn't have a hospital if no one lived there.* Then came the difficult situation: How would I tell mother where we were moving to? I had lived in the United States for almost four years and had never heard about Milwaukee. How could I expect Mother to know the city I was talking about? The closest city to Milwaukee that is known to people abroad is Chicago, so I wrote Mother a letter and I told her that we were moving to a city near Chicago. I received a letter back from her, the translation of which follows:

My beloved daughter Mary,
I wish to send you lots of love, longing to see you in the near future.

You told me in your last letter that you are moving to the land of gangs. The city of Al Capone. Don't do this, Mary. Don't do it to yourself and to your mother.

America is a vast country, there must be some other place for you to go. Some better place to make a living. Think about it and think very seriously, then let me know your decision.

May you remain for ever dear and loved,

Your Mother,
Josephine

This is not only my mother's conception of Chicago, but it is the bell that rings in everyone's mind when the name Chicago is mentioned. How could I blame Mother, or anyone who didn't live in the States, for not understanding the reality of America when people who live here don't quite understand?

I could not absorb the size of the land, and the differences in each state. Its nature, its government, its agriculture, its laws. The fact that each state is almost like an independent country: connected to other states on its borders, but unlike those of countries, the borders are not policed.

Not until I started looking into Milwaukee, by reading everything that was written and listening to everything that was said about the city, did I start to appreciate the size of the United States of America. I listened to the sports news about Milwaukee, the dairy products news, read about what it was known for: its beer, and of course, the distance between it and the largest city close by, Chicago. I had visited Chicago about two years earlier, and I knew what a lovely city it was and how wonderful the Magnificent Mile is. Now I learned that O'Hare International Airport is the busiest airport in the United States, and that it is less than one hundred miles south of Milwaukee. This was an important factor for us since we like to, and need to, travel internationally.

As the time got closer for our move from Hartford to Milwaukee, on June 30, 1973, it was necessary that we make a trip to Wisconsin to find where we would live when we moved. We booked a room at a hotel downtown, rented a car, and drove by Lake Michigan. Milwaukee looked good, peaceful, and inviting:

> I traveled North,
> I traveled South,
> I even went from East to West.
> It's only here
> The Lake is clear,
> The deer are dear,
> The beer is chilled
> For every guest.

We asked the advice of locals about areas to live. Shorewood was the suitable place, and we wanted to be near the lake and not too far from downtown. We rented an apartment on Murray Avenue. When the weekend was over, we flew back to Hartford.

The apartment we occupied in Hartford had to be vacated a day or so before the first day of July. The building managers needed time to get our apartment painted for the new tenants. And the new tenants needed to be able to move in before they started their training at the hospital on the first of July. So timing was tight.

The apartment also was scheduled to be checked before we moved, so that any damage would be taken care of. I expected to be informed of the day they would come to inspect the apartment, but instead I received a note telling me that the apartment had been inspected and everything was fine. I was upset that people had been in our apartment without my knowledge. I felt that they had handled our lives as if we were their property.

Preparations for the move had to start early. We called moving companies to find the least expensive one. The moving company would have had to pick up our furniture at the end of June and store it for two months. We were going to drive from Hartford to Milwaukee with our personal belongings, drop them off, leave the car, and fly to Egypt to visit with our families for two months, then return to Milwaukee in time for Gamil to start work at the VA Hospital in September—at which time I would have to arrange the apartment and start preparing for the arrival of our baby in November.

To make matters a little bit more complex, but fun, we decided to visit England to see my sister and my brother on our way to Egypt. We also planned on stopping in Paris for three days. This was 1973, and we were now legal U.S. immigrants, not aliens anymore! But that wasn't enough to allow us entry into those countries without visas. We were still carrying Egyptian passports; therefore we needed visas. While still in Hartford, I started my trips once again to New York City for those two visas. Moving day came before the visas were granted. I was told that the British consulate in New York would send the approval to the Chicago consulate to grant us the visas.

The moving company promised us they would pick up our furniture on one of the last three days in the month. When the first day of the last three days went by and they did not show up, and the same thing happened the second day, we began to worry about our situation. On the third day, I called the company first thing in the morning. I was told the movers would be there sometime that day. We had errands to run, so Gamil and I had to alternate; one would stay at home waiting for the movers, while the other one ran the errands. At 11:00 A.M., I called the company and a Mr. Brenner answered:

MARY: May I talk to the person handling the Khairs' moving, please?
MR. BRENNER: This is he.
MARY: When will the truck come to take our furniture?
MR. BRENNER: The first truck that pulls in, we'll send to your home.
MARY: Thank you.

12:00 noon, talking to Mr. Brenner once again:

MARY: Has any truck pulled in yet?
MR. BRENNER: The men are unloading it, and they will be there as soon as they are done. This job is giving me gray hair. (A piece of information I did not care to know)

At 1:00 P.M. I called to ask Mr. Brenner once more:

MARY: Is the truck unloaded and ready to be sent our way yet?
MR. BRENNER: The men are eating lunch.

2:00 P.M. Apparently, Mr. Brenner forgot what he had said earlier.

MARY: When will you send us the truck?
MR. BRENNER: The first truck to pull in I will send over to your home.

That was when I believed my suspicions and decided to add a few more gray hairs to Mr. Brenner's head.

MARY: But Mr. Brenner, that was what you told me at eleven o'clock, and at twelve noon. You said the men were unloading the truck. At one o'clock you said they were eating lunch. Tell me now, what would you like me to believe?

MR. BRENNER: Before the sun sets, a truck will have moved your furniture but I can't tell you a certain time. I will call you when they are on their way.

MARY: My phone will be disconnected after this call.

MR. BRENNER: I'll call you at your neighbor's.

MARY: My neighbors moved already. Mr. Brenner, I will tell you what I'll do. If your truck doesn't show up, I will shove the furniture out the window and get myself out of here before they come and shove me out the door.

This was how my last conversation with Mr. Brenner ended. I then put the last items in boxes, a job the movers were contracted to do from beginning to end, and I was ready for the next step. They finally showed up, but the sun had already set, and that was a summer day in June.

The next day we loaded our car, gathered our maps, and headed west, starting the long drive to Milwaukee.

4
Leaving the East Coast for the Midwest

We arrived at the hotel in Ohio shortly after midnight, very tired after the long drive. The next morning, we started our drive early, heading west. After a couple of hours of driving, we stopped for a midmorning break, then started on our way again. I was reading the AAA's Trip-tik (their personalized map packet) but I was reading it backward and we soon realized we were returning east!

We stopped at a bar to get some directions. An elderly man sitting at the counter sipping his beer helped us. I happened to notice that the amount of beer and the shape of his glass, as well as the way he spoke, seemed unique.

We returned to the car and looked over our maps to get our directions straight, then got on the road once again, heading west this time. After about an hour, we stopped for lunch in the small town of Medina, Ohio. The place looked exactly like the one where we had asked for directions earlier but we were sure this had to be a coincidence.

We walked in and sat at a table, then we looked up at the counter—only to see a man who looked the same as the earlier one, with the same drink, the same glass, and even the same amount of beer in his glass. We asked each other if he could be the same man. We were sure it was not the same place, even though everything looked the same. We spoke in Arabic so that no one would be aware of our confusion. Could we be caught in a whirlwind, not heading forward or backward, east or west? Then came the voice from the counter asking, "Did you find your way west yet?" We could not believe our ears. As much as we both wanted to ask him how he had gotten there before us and resumed his very same position, we were both overwhelmed by the situation and we just answered his question, "Yes."

We arrived in Milwaukee late in the day, and the first thing I wanted to do the following morning was to call the British consulate in Chicago to find out about our visas. Gamil's approval was there, but not mine. That raised a question in my mind. I wondered if it could be because in 1968 I had gone to England and gotten a job without the government's approval? Yet, I reminded myself, I had been to England several times since then. . . . A day later my worries were eliminated; my application for the visa was accepted. Then we had to go to Chicago to have our passports stamped. We also had to go to the French consulate, where we were granted visas as well.

We took off on our trip two days after arriving in Milwaukee, our first stop being England to visit family, then off to Paris where we stayed at Hotel Ascot near the Paris L'Opera. As close to it as we were, we could only marvel at what a magnificent piece of architectural engineering it was. We walked around it from outside only, but even that "tour" was a feast for the eyes. We also walked down the Champs-Élysées, climbed the Eiffel Tower, and ate a delicious dinner, the name of which I fail to recall, but I have photographs of it. We took the elevator up the Arc de Triomphe and had a good look at the star-shaped city of Paris, where the streets looked like beams of light radiating from the center of the star.

PARIS

Your name awakens all our senses,
Your magic never ceases.
We cruise the Seine
And climb the Eiffel Tower.

In the morning, a star shining bright.
At night, "The City of Light."
Your architectural power?
Your manicured gardens?
Beauty, our eyes devour.
Paris, you are
The cradle of art
And history, engraved
By Napoléon Bonaparte.

In every country we visited, during that trip or on previous trips, a piece of Egyptian history was related by the tour guide. For example in France, the ancient Egyptian obelisk adorning the Place de la Concorde in the center of Paris, and in the case of Venice, Italy, the tour guide pointed out where the remains of St. Mark, the saint who introduced Christianity to Egypt, were buried. This made us feel very proud of our heritage.

In our short visit to the Paris area, we also visited Sacre Coeur, Napoléon's Les Invalides (the army museum where Napoléon is buried), Chateau de Malmaison, the Louvre, Versailles, Fontainebleau Palace and we strolled through the Tuileries gardens.

The three days in Paris were over and we headed to Orly International Airport to board Air France to Cairo. The flight was to stop in Rome, then continue on to Egypt. About halfway to Rome, an announcement told us that we were headed back to Orly because of a malfunction with a part in the plane. Passengers were in a panic. We refused to believe the announcement but that did not change the fact; we returned to Orly.

The plane started circling the airport; the flight engineer came down the aisle and tore up the carpeting, uncovering a metal part beneath it. We could see him reach in and unscrew some parts of the body of the plane. I could not imagine what he was doing, but later I was told that he had drained the fuel tank to minimize the chance of fire upon landing. Had I known this at the time, I would have been even more scared.

A young man across the aisle from me started yelling hysterically. The crew tried to help him but he just couldn't calm down. As the plane got lower, I saw fire engines, ambulances, and teams of professionals surrounding an area outside the fence. I was amazed at how the crew could keep so calm under such pressing circumstances.

We did land safely and exited using the stairs brought to the emergency exit. We were at an isolated end of the airport, though, not the normal departure area, so we had to walk all the way back to the passenger's lounge. There we were told to wait. We did not know at the time whether it would be a few minutes or a few hours. We had no French francs to buy food, and we could not sit back and relax because we expected them to call on us any second to board the plane. The trip was taking its toll on me. I was swollen all over.

Night came and we still had no word. The hours grew deeper into the night; we got more and more hungry, tired, and restless. Finally, when we thought they had forgotten about us, we were invited to the dining room for a hot meal. All the passengers walked in and sat at the tables, and were ready to eat. I picked up the fork and knife, the aroma was more than inviting, as hungry as we were. I cut the first slice of chicken, raised the fork, and attempted to open my mouth to devour my first bite when the flight attendant walked in, and in a nervous tone of voice said, "All passengers of Air France going to Cairo please board your flight at gate number eighteen immediately." It was the word *immediately* that made me place the fork back on the plate rather than in my mouth. We left to board the plane as instructed.

We arrived in Cairo safely at some odd hour of the very early morning. Nevertheless, our families were at the airport awaiting our arrival. Gamil's brothers were there, and so were my sisters. Isis had come from England and Samia from Bahrain only a few days ahead of us. The family had arranged a trip to a resort area that was very dear to our hearts: Mersa Matrouh, northwest of Cairo, west of Alexandria, on the Mediterranean Sea.

The beach there is known for its silky white sand and clear turquoise waters. It is recorded in the history books as the place where Mark Antony and Cleopatra settled. There is a large lagoon west of the harbor named Cleopatra's Bath, an ancient artistic piece of nature, which stands like a giant rock in the middle of the clear water. The white powdery texture of the sand is seen through the water in the shallow areas; as the water gets deeper, the turquoise color does too and the whitish sand disappears. The beach is not polluted by oil and grease like that of Alexandria, since Mersa Matrouh is not a commercial harbor. The Lido Hotel, where we were to stay, overlooks the beach. Perfectly located, it is an old, well-kept hotel.

Mersa Matrouh is so dear to our hearts because my father was assigned to work there when he got his first job with the Egyptian federal government. When he and my mother got married, she had to leave her parents, who lived in the center of the busy city of Cairo, to join my father in the desert resort area of Mersa Matrouh. The city itself is a sandy desert, but the northernmost part is on the beautiful Mediterranean Sea. Mother had to travel by train from Cairo to Alexandria, a distance of one hundred and thirty-five miles, then take the boat from Alexandria's harbor an equal distance to get to Mersa Matrouh. There was no airport to make this a smoother trip at the time. For my mother, leaving Cairo to live in Mersa Matrouh was similar to my having to leave home and all my cousins and friends to live in the United States.

My sister Isis and my brother, Samir, were born when the family lived in Mersa Matrouh, and they attended a Greek school there for the first year or two of their education.

My middle sister, Samia, and I were born and grew up in Cairo after my parents had moved back. We always heard stories about life in that resort city and about the home they lived in then, as well as about the friends they made and the Greek school they attended. So this trip was our opportunity to see what we'd heard so much about.

It brought back memories for Mother and for Isis, and it made things concrete for Samia and me. To make things even better, the manager recognized us by name. He presented us with the rooms we wanted, even though it was the busy season and we had no previous reservations. We met a couple of old family friends and we went to visit them, a rerun of activities for Mother and Isis, and playing the role for Samia and me.

When it was time to leave Mersa Matrouh for Cairo, then on to the United States, Mother joined us. We needed her to help us prepare for the arrival of our first child.

It was the end of August when we arrived at the apartment in Shorewood. We opened the door to find that the movers had delivered our furniture as planned while we were away, and the cartons were all over the place, from floor to ceiling and from wall to wall. Heavy housework was awaiting us. It took a few days to get the apartment in shape, then we started shopping and preparing for the arrival of the baby in November. The most challenging thing was trying to find a name for the baby that would be pronounced the same in English as in Arabic, and that would be familiar to both cultures. This took some research and I finally came up with the name Carmen for a girl and Samy for a boy. Every letter in those names is pronounced the same by the speakers of both languages, and the opera *Carmen* made that name known all over the world. On November 14, 1973, Carmen Mary was born.

Having just moved to Milwaukee, we did not have any friends to share the joy with, so we shared it among the three of us and the baby. Eventually, through an Egyptian doctor at the hospital where Gamil worked, we were introduced to another Egyptian family and our circle of acquaintances started to expand. The same thing that happened in New York in 1969 through 1971 happened again in Milwaukee. Our small group of Egyptian Christians gathered together and rented a church on Saturday evenings to pray. The priest from Chicago, where there was a larger community of Egyptians, Father Marcus Bishay, came regularly to Milwaukee for service. Carmen was baptized one Saturday evening, and that was a happy event that we shared as a small community. She was the kind of baby every parent wished to have. She loved the outdoors and always made me proud to have her as my child. I was often asked, "How come your baby never cries?"

We enjoyed watching Carmen grow, and I spent all my time with her, which made me very happy. I would never have wanted my life any other way. It was a different pace, however, from racing to get to work on time, working hard all day, and at the end of the day going home and unwinding. This new life with a child included being alert and ready to respond at all hours of the day and night, and on weekends, and during vacations.

The Egyptian community in Chicago was growing constantly; therefore, they were able to afford to purchase a church. They did, and we started to go to St. Marks' Church in Roselle, Illinois—105 miles from Milwaukee—to pray, whenever it was possible for us to go on a Sunday. Father Marcus Bishay was still our priest.

Christmas and Easter started to feel more like they used to when we lived in Egypt, because the group celebrated them together in our traditional ways. We made friends in Chicago and spent special times in their company. We were never sure, however, come Easter, if the church would be able to provide us with palms on Palm Sunday. The palms we were used to were bigger than those used by Western churches, and had to be specially ordered. We wanted to be able to celebrate the way the Church in Egypt did.

Little girls and boys go to church all dressed up, carrying their full-size palms, woven in a variety of shapes and decorated with flowers. Some looked like a heart, others slim and sort of braided close to the stem—every different artistic presentation. We wanted our children to be able to enjoy this feast the way we did when we were their age. Would the Midwest provide them with the warm look of the palms?

> THE PALM AT THE END OF OUR ARM
> Here in the Midwest
> Rainwaters flood and flood,
> Palm trees are not to be found.
> Here comes Easter Sunday,
> Preceded by Palm Sunday,
> And every year we wonder:
> Will it be the palm at the end of our arm?
> Or will the shipment make it from yonder?

Every year our anxiety proved to be unfounded. The palms arrived in good time for us to weave, braid, and celebrate!

We had to learn how to dress for the weather in Milwaukee and to find our way around the city. As Carmen approached her first birthday, once again my inner call to go back to graduate school got louder and louder. The setting of our community was perfect for me. The University of Wisconsin-Milwaukee was within a few miles of where we lived, and the Shorewood Public Library was across the street from the apartment building. To make things even better, a retired, loving lady called Mrs.

Ransom lived two floors down, and she loved to baby-sit Carmen. Things could not get any better, and I was eager to try once again to go for my master's degree.

I contacted the university and was told that I would have to go through the international department to evaluate the records I had brought with me from Egypt, and I would have to take an English-language test. I was very serious about my plans. I took the test and passed, and I presented every required piece of paper. After all that, I received a letter of apology telling me that I was not accepted for graduate education.

I called the English department and asked to meet with the chairman. When it was time for my appointment, as I left home, I told my visiting mother that I was not going to argue their decision, but to defend my education. My quest was to make it known that Egyptians are educated and can speak the English language, understand it and even write it.

Mr. Sappenfield was a much kinder person than I had thought the chairman would be. After an interesting and rewarding conversation, he felt that I knew the English language well enough to be accepted for receiving the education I was seeking at his institution. In fact, by the end of the visit, we were discussing what courses would be better for me than others. After that meeting, I received a letter of acceptance in the mail and I was delighted that my wish was on its way to becoming reality.

In January 1975 I started my first course, in drama, my favorite area of literature. I soon found that this was the wrong choice and that Mr. Sappenfield's advice had been accurate. The drama professor did not think that I was able to write papers, even though he said that I knew my literary work. With his help, I switched to an independent writing course with Professor Replogle. This helped me acquire the ability to write the lengthy papers expected of a student here in the United States.

My second course was taught by Professor Harrold. He enjoyed what he taught and had an interest in each student and their individual pursuits, and that showed in how he was always happy and more than willing to help with information and research material. When he asked a student, "How are you doing?" he asked with a keen sense of care and concern that was obvious in the tone of the question—unlike the manner in which this question is commonly asked, often without even waiting for a response. This gave me a sense of importance as a student and encouraged me to seek help to improve my work.

I continued to take one course every semester and work as hard as I could on lengthening my papers; a practice that is contrary to my previous training where "precise and concise" was the best way to present a piece of work. We always had to answer questions to the point without the introductions and lengthy endings.

The family was also a challenge, with a growing child. During the second half of 1976, I had to drop out of a course because I was unable to keep up with the amount of reading while expecting our second child. I did not have enough energy to maintain our home, my schoolwork, and my health, especially when I came down with a bad cold and could not read for two days. By the time I was well enough to read again, I was too far behind to catch up with the class, so I dropped out.

On March 6, 1977, Nancy Isis was born, a healthy, happy, and very good baby. She slept through the night at four weeks of age and ate three meals a day like an adult when she was three months old. But she never liked to go out. She was the exact opposite of her older sister, who calmed down only when we took her out.

When Nancy was about six weeks old, the Coptic Orthodox Christian Pope, Shenouda III, came from Egypt to visit the Egyptian Christian immigrants of the See of St. Mark and to attend to their ecclesiastical needs. This was the first time ever in history for the Pope to visit the United States, where the congregation has been growing in number. That happened in May 1977, and we wanted to have Nancy baptized on this historic event, even though she was not yet the eight weeks old that tradition dictates. With the help of some friends we quickly arranged for it and joined a rather large group of parents baptizing their little babies.

My literature courses were still on hold. We found that staying in our apartment with two children was practically impossible from all aspects. The building was occupied by senior citizens, who almost went into a panic when they saw a child, let alone a baby. We were also getting very crowded, and it was inconvenient to stay any longer in the apartment. It seemed that buying a house would be a solution to the space problem, but Gamil was not yet sure if he would be staying in Wisconsin for a while, or if taking a job elsewhere in a year or so would be better for his career. We didn't want to buy a house, then sell it within a short time, as we would be sure to lose money that way.

What we were really trying to do was answer a question about the future, which is impossible to do. In this indecisive situation, we turned to our friends for advice.

In my own heart and mind I was also concerned about whether or not I would be able to continue my graduate education if we moved elsewhere. I felt that I had finally placed myself where I wanted to be after being so patient and waiting for years to get to where I was.

With the help of our friends, we realized that Milwaukee now felt like our second home; the children had been born there, and that meant a lot to us. We decided to stay in Milwaukee, to buy a house, and to let the future dictate what would happen next.

The hunting for a house began. Mother was visiting to help with the second child, and now her help reached yet another level. She was needed to watch the children for lengthy bits of time while I went with the real estate agent to check out houses.

During these continued jaunts, I was told the history of Shorewood in particular, since we wanted to continue to live there. I learned that Shorewood is one of the oldest areas in Milwaukee; that people came from the South and built summer homes by the lake for their vacations. The reason I wanted to stay in Shorewood was to be able to continue with my education, but we wanted a house that was newly built and that did not match with the location. Therefore, we had to give up and look for a new house away from Shorewood.

We made a number of unsuccessful attempts to find a suitable home, but there were problems with each one: one was in a flood area, another's backyard was sitting on a school playground. One day we saw a couple of houses advertised in the paper that sounded like what we wanted. That same day the real estate agent called and asked to show me a couple of houses. I decided to go and have a look at them with her. If I liked them, then Gamil would look at them in the evening after work. She quoted the prices over the phone to me. I liked one of the houses—the one on Marigold Court—very much.

It was as good as its description. The big window in the living room not only allowed a generous amount of sunshine in from the east to brighten the house, it resembled a wide-angle lens to view the openness and the beauty of nature outside. I noticed there was a little carpet nonchalantly thrown over the sign advertising the sale of the house, but I didn't give this matter much attention.

In the evening, we went back with Gamil to have a look at the house, and he liked it too. We got in our car and followed the agent, headed toward her office. But before we got to our destination she got out of her car at a red traffic light and came over to us and said, "My friend lives right here. Rather than go all the way to the office, we can stop at her house and fill out the forms. She has some at her home." We agreed.

We were warmly welcomed by her friend, and shown a brand-new car in the garage. The two friends had a brief side conference, then we sat at the table to complete and sign our deal. Everything seemed to be going smoothly until we got to the price of the house. She gave us a price that was three thousand dollars over what she had quoted me over the phone. Then she implied that if we didn't accept that price, the house we liked so much after all that searching would never be ours.

Unhappy about what she was doing to us, and uncomfortable about the situation we were placed in, we signed the contract, knowing that there was cause for the lack of peace of mind. On our way home, we remembered the ad in the paper about a house being sold by the owner, not by a real estate agency, at a price even less than what she had quoted over the phone in the morning, let alone the evening price. We thought it might be the same house.

With that in mind, we went home and searched for the paper. It *was* the very same house. The real estate agent must have contacted the owner and arranged to bring us to see the house, then led us to believe that her agency was selling it. That explained the little carpet covering the sign when I had gone in the morning, which really said FOR SALE BY OWNER. And it also explained why the sign had been removed when we'd gone back that evening.

We called the agent right away, to face her with what she has done to us. There was no answer all that night.

Dejected, we went to sleep, and at 6:30 A.M. the following morning, we gave her a call. She was half asleep, confused. With a voice filled with fear she tried to defend her deed, but she ended up begging us to leave her alone or she would lose her job. She called me later on in the day to tell me that we should go ahead and buy the house from the owner and that she would stay out of the whole matter. She expressed concern once again about her job and that we might sue her and the company. I assured her that we were not after her losing her job or getting her in any trouble with the law, we just wanted to buy the house and have no problems surrounding the purchase.

We realized then that we would need an attorney, and although we had never consulted one before on any matter at all, we knew we were not going to be able to handle this situation the way it should be handled. Our neighbor was an attorney, so we asked him to help us with the purchase of that house. His first request was a written letter from the Realty office stating that they had nothing to do with the sale or purchase of the given property. The letter was issued and the steps to purchase the house started to take the normal path.

The owner of the house then said to us, "Boy, I knew that woman would be in trouble if the buyer saw the ad in the paper. It was the first time she saw the house, and she was showing it to you as if she had been here before." He did not even know what had happened the evening before at her friend's house.

All is well that ends well, as the saying goes. We bought the house and moved in on July 27, 1977. Carmen was three and a half years old and Nancy a little over four months old. Mother was still with us. We needed to look into preschools in the area. The neighbors were the most important support we needed, and as the Arabic saying goes, "Check out your neighbor before checking out the house." I was concerned, however, as to whether we, as foreigners, were going to be accepted in the neighborhood. This concern was eliminated very quickly. All the residents on the court warmly welcomed us.

Marigold Court turned out to be the perfect model of friendship and unity. I was given lists of telephone numbers of every place, business, emergency, schools, baby-sitters, and anything one might need. Each neighbor had either a daughter or two, or even three. All the children on the court were girls close in age to each other, and all became friends, both children and parents.

MARIGOLD COURT

A crescent reflecting that of the moon,
Echoing its peace in a court of friendship.
Merry we were, gold our memories.
Marianne, Lisa, and Fran
Were to guard:
Carmen, Jenny, and Kristin,
Kara, Nancy, and Karin.
The roots dug deep,
And sprouted joy.
The Band-Aids were placed
To soothe hurt egos,
Then removed to bring smiles
On our little angels' faces.
Now teach us and treat us
And guide us to success.
The marigolds have spread,
From coast to coast,
Gathered at the stems
Like a bouquet full of life,
Blossomed to shine,
From East to West.

The responsibility of the big house, two little children, and the cost to maintain all this started to be felt quickly. We attempted to decorate the house a bit. Mother's visa was about to expire, since guests are permitted to stay a given length of time in the country they are visiting, so she left us for England to visit my sister and brother there. At the same time, we were studying American history and government to take our citizenship examination. All the studying paid off. We were sworn in as American citizens in August 1977.

While in court, one of the newly sworn citizens at the celebration that followed the oath asked us where we were from. I told him, and he then asked us if we have been to see King Tut. I did not know what he was talking about for a second because I had never heard the name shortened before. Then I told him that we had not been to see the exhibit. I thought to myself: *Why should we visit the exhibit here when we saw the tomb in Luxor, and why do people in this country like to shorten every name?* I heard a young immigrant recently, on a television program, answer a reporter's question as to whether he likes Americans. He gave her an answer that I liked: He said that he likes Americans but that they had changed his name:

FOR THE LOVE OF THEIR FIRST NAME

Mike, Mitch, Al, and Ed,
Sue, Jan, Kate, and Jen.
Phil, Tim, Sam, and Ben,
Barb, De, Val, and Kim.
I love Americans,
Said a young immigrant,
But they changed my name.
At home they call me Richard
Over here they call me Dick!

As for King Tutankhamen, I felt that his name should not be shortened:

ON TOUR

I got the key,
I got the door,
Where is he to adore?
Where is all the gold?
Where is Grandpa?
"On Tour," they say,
"King Tut is on tour."

King Tut they call him?!
Cut short his name?
They got the Tut,
I got the rest,
Tutankhamen is his full name.

As the children started to grow up, our trips to Chicago on Sundays became more and more regular. This was the practical way for Carmen and Nancy to receive their religious, as well as their cultural, education among the people from our home country who were raising families under similar conditions.

5
Living as a U.S. Citizen

We were very happy with our newly acquired American citizenship and the fact that our children were now first-generation Americans. We had bought our first house in a suburb and a second car for the growing family. But all this bliss was outweighed by the delight of acquiring a U.S. passport. That document would allow us to travel freely; no visas would be required now, when we went to visit almost any country we might wish to see. And when we arrived at our destination we would no longer have to answer such dehumanizing questions as: "Why are you here?" "How long will you stay?" "How much money do you have?"

I did not waste another semester out of school. I returned to my graduate courses at the University of Wisconsin-Milwaukee and continued to work as hard as I possibly could. As I got closer to completion, I needed help with the children even more than ever before. Once again my mother came to the rescue. In May of 1979 I received my master's degree, four years after I started working on it but ten years after my first attempt to start in New York. After graduation, my plan was to take my family and travel to England and Egypt. That way we could keep mother company on her return trip after all her help. We planned to leave for England a week before Gamil was free to go, and spend that week with my sister Isis. Then we would all fly to Egypt together.

Wrapped in the joy of my recently achieved master's degree and of my traveling for the first time with the new U.S. passport, topped by the proud feeling of bringing home two lovely children to show to the extended family, we took off from O'Hare. Never did the thought of Mother's passport being Egyptian cross our minds.

As we neared England, passengers were handed a card and asked to fill it out before landing. It was from British Immigration, and one of the questions was about the traveler's citizenship. On all my previous trips I had filled in that line with *Egyptian*, but this time I knew I had to write *American*. It was much harder to do than I would have thought: It felt as if I were trying to get away with some big lie.

I looked around me to see if anyone was watching what I was about to write, then I fixed my eyes on the line in my passport that confirmed my U.S. citizenship, to assure myself that I was not lying and that no one would call out: "You are not American." I told myself that it was only my inner voice giving me trouble. But I found that it was also a moment of transition for me: Was writing *American* denying my heritage? It felt like a tug-of-war between two very strong forces in me: I did not want to deny who I had been since birth, but at the same time I was very happy to travel with my two daughters as an American citizen.

When we landed at Heathrow I presented our passports to the immigration officer with all the confidence in the world. He looked at my passport and the children's and welcomed us to his country. Then he looked at Mother's passport, flipped through it page by page, and then from back to front since Arabic is read from right to left. With an angry tone and look he said twice, "No visa. No visa." I felt as if I'd been hit by a hammer right on my head. His words left me speechless. As if in a nightmare, here I was with my mother, unable to produce the required visa I'd forgotten to apply for.

All I could do was explain the facts. I told him that I was traveling with my U.S. passport for the first time and that I had been so happy I didn't have to apply for a visa anymore that I'd forgotten about Mother's. Also, I explained how busy I'd been, working on my master's degree and taking care of the children. Mother's visa, unfortunately, had not even entered my mind.

He said he had to meet with his boss about the matter, so he got up, put his jacket on, and took the documents in to his boss's office. We were left waiting, wondering if Mother would be allowed to enter the country or if she would have to board the next flight leaving England for Egypt?

When he came out of his boss's office, he said that this time they would let her in because she had recently been there, but that they would never again allow it to happen. We thanked him and gratefully carried on with our entry.

Our trip, after all, was a success. We had a great time in both England and Egypt, and we returned to the United States to carry on with raising our young family.

Carmen graduated from preschool and went on to elementary school, and Nancy was old enough to follow in her sister's footsteps. My role was to help the teachers at school and to be involved as a parent in the education of my children. As I tended regularly to my volunteer commitments, I had the opportunity to observe the teaching techniques and how different they were from the days when I had gone to school.

For example, the method of teaching by using props or games was almost unknown to me before I was asked to play cards with small groups of children. When I asked what playing cards would do (because I thought it was only a waste of time for me and for the children), my attention was directed to the math skills involved in that game. In my day we were handed a sheet of paper filled with mathematical equations to practice at home.

Another form of hands-on education that was interesting to me was the frequent use of field trips. When I was a student, we would go on one trip during the school year and that was always toward the end of the year, as a reward for our hard work. We always looked forward to that trip, and although all trips are educational, we considered ours to be strictly recreational. In America I came to see the benefits of going on frequent field trips by going on many of them. I went with my daughters' classes to a hospital and saw how the children, after applying plaster to one another's fingers, learned that it's not frightening to go to hospital when the need arises. A trip to the pumpkin farm taught me what I lacked in agricultural knowledge with regard to pumpkins. I learned, for example, that at the time of planting them, the seeds are placed in groups called hills, not singly like other plants. Also, that they are not harvested until the skin is tough, and that is about one hundred and twenty days after seeding.

The use of videos, slides, and movies was another reason for me to be initially surprised, but then I came to understand how useful visual presentations can be. The most sophisticated of all props came to the classroom when Carmen was in third grade: the king of all props, The Computer.

Hands-on equipment certainly captures the attention, heightens interest, and teaches in an easy-to-digest manner, rather than the bitter pills of written exercises and memorization that we had to swallow, dose after dose, until we graduated. But nothing beats the joy of creative writing and the lessons one learns from that. When Carmen was in fourth grade, her writing teacher asked the class to write a poem about Martin Luther King Jr. I was driving her home from school when I heard her puffing in the backseat. I asked her, "What's wrong, Carmen?" She said, "I have to write a poem and I don't know how to start it." I attempted to help her, saying,

> "Red and yellow,
> Black and white,
> Martin Luther
> Wanted to unite."

She quickly said, "Okay, okay, that's all I need."

When we got home, she ran up to her room, and closed her door. A few minutes later she came downstairs and asked if I wanted to hear what she had written. I must admit that I learned a lot from her poem. It was full of information I had never learned about his life and his thought, and the poem was written beautifully. After reading it she asked me if she might change the choice of colors. Black and white, she said, were the colors of people, but why had I chosen red and yellow? I told her that I thought we shouldn't change those colors, because they too were the colors of some people. I took that opportunity to tell her about the other races of the world.

In our home Gamil and I spoke Arabic, and so did Carmen until she was about four years old. Except for the English words she picked up from watching Sesame Street, all her vocabulary was Arabic. When we moved to our new house and she started to play with the neighbors' children, she had to speak English. Sometimes when she was outside playing, she would run in the house to ask me how to say a word in English, and then she would go out once again to continue her conversation or her story.

One day she had the refrigerator door open and she was just standing there, neither taking anything out nor closing it. I asked her to close the door, and I said it in English. There was no response. This was unlike Carmen; she was a good child who always listened to what she was told. I got all upset and repeated my request in Arabic, and she responded by closing the refrigerator door right away. I realized then that language in our home needed attention.

I remembered the day I'd gone to Donges Bay School to register Carmen for kindergarten. I had to fill out a form. One of the questions on the form was: "Do you speak any language other than English at home?" I did not think anything wrong with the question and I answered, of course, "Yes, Arabic." Then I overheard two mothers discussing that question. It baffled them that a language other than English could be spoken. They wondered aloud, "What language do they think we speak at home? Dirty?" I was shocked at the lack of awareness some people suffer toward the rest of the world. I thought that by the time people become parents, they should know better.

Another incident happened when Carmen was in first grade. When she came home after school one day, she attempted to tell me about her school day. She started to relate what a boy named Matt had brought for show-and-tell. The word *mat* in Arabic means "he died." It must be that my brain was in the Arabic mode when she started her story; our conversation went as follows:

MARY: So, tell me about your school today.
CARMEN: A boy, Matt—

Here I interrupted her in a state of panic and a higher tone:

MARY: *Mat?* Today? In class? What did the teacher do?
CARMEN (looking at me with confusion and a subdued tone compared to earlier): Nothing, Mom, I was going to tell you what he brought for show-and-tell because it was very special.

I realized then that "Matt" was the boy's name. I tried to calm myself down to listen to her story but I was so shaken, it took me a long time to get back to normal, and we never enjoyed the events of that day.

TONGUES

From right to left
And left to right
I read and write.
And when it's time to reach my God,
I switch to yet another tongue,
For Coptic is the voice of prayer.
As for French, forget the grammaire!
In English, I will write my verse.
In Arabic, I like to converse.

It took a lot of hurt feelings, misunderstandings, and what seemed like impolite interruptions before we were able to almost perfect conducting the two languages simultaneously at home without causing too many problems.

Another adjustment I had to deal with was the food choices for the children. The difference in the cuisine between Egyptians and Americans was something to learn to understand. Peanut butter was unknown to me; I knew peanuts as nuts only. Hot dogs I knew as sausages; macaroni was always dressed with tomato sauce and ground beef, not with cheese. When the children wanted to eat lunch with their friends, I had to satisfy everyone's palate. All the moms in the neighborhood helped me make this happen. My Egyptian cooking was placed on the back burner and I catered to the children's youthful tastes. I believe food is always a fun experience, and I learned a lot about the difference in cultural palates:

THE CULTURAL PALATE

Slab the peanut butter on Mrs. Karl's
Spread the jelly,
Bite, chew, swallow?
My mouth is Poli-Gripped.
"Wash it down with soda."

My kitchen is aflame with aroma,
Of spicy kebab, minty chicken, cinnamony dessert,
That soothes the senses,
Glides with glee down the throat
To meet a stomach whose juices were aroused,
Awaiting the arrival of a glutton's satisfaction.
No soda, milk, or juicy drink
Is called upon to wash this down.

Yet, children want to be like those
Who eat their hot dogs, and God knows.
"You cook American?" asks my neighbor.
"No, traditional is on my table."
Our taste buds frolic on a bridge
Created by joy, food brings.

In Egypt we ate a full breakfast before leaving for school or work. A standard morning meal would be cheese and eggs, or fava beans dressed with oil, salt, pepper, and lemon juice. We drank hot tea, with milk or plain. Egyptians finished up their breakfast with marmalade, honey, or any one of the various homemade jams made from fruits such as figs, dates, or lareng (similar to oranges but with a more bitter bite). This complete meal carried the person all the way until lunchtime, which would be between 2:00 and 3:00 P.M., except for maybe a cup of espresso coffee during the midmorning hours. As for schoolchildren, they ate a small sandwich during their midmorning break at 10:00 A.M. The sandwiches, traditionally, were made of pita bread filled with feta cheese. Sometimes slices of cucumber dressed with a little salt and powdered dried mint were added for extra appetizing flavor. Mint was often added to the food; or sometimes it was boiled and served like hot tea for its soothing digestive effect.

Lunch was our main meal; as dinner is in the Western countries. The family was gathered; the food was placed on the dinner table in the center; and everyone would help themselves.

As for the menu, a standard everyday one would consist of either meat or chicken, the meat usually lamb or beef, sometimes veal; a vegetable; rice or macaroni; salad greens and tomatoes. Dessert was always fruit. The meat was sometimes prepared as shish kebab, roast, or thin steak treated with spices—among them mint, garlic, lemon juice, beaten eggs, milk, and bread crumbs. Such a steak is called *buftake*. The chicken was also served in a variety of ways. It could be grilled, baked, stuffed with *ferik* (bulghur), or boiled and lightly fried. Occasionally it was deboned. Chicken and meat spices varied within the ones mentioned earlier, and some others were nutmeg, allspice, coriander, and cardamom. As for the choices of vegetables, okra topped the list of a lot of Egyptian meals, as did *molokhia* (a green soupy dish), and *khobeiza* (a green leafy vegetable cut very thin, liquified, and poured into the boiling broth of turkey, chicken, or a dark meat to cook for a few minutes). Garlic sauce was prepared to pour over the *molokhia* and it was served right away. All the other vegetables were the familiar ones such as zucchini, green beans, peas, and eggplant (prepared as *mousaka* with ground beef and tomato sauce). All the vegetables, except for the green soupy ones such as *khobeiza* and *molokhia*, were cooked in tomato sauce. Sometimes ground beef was added as well. The standard rice was white, and it was served plain. There were fancier gourmet dishes that combined rice with nuts and giblets, or that mixed noodles with the rice. The salad was made up of lettuce, tomatoes, cucumber, green pepper, and green onions (optional). The dressing was always vegetable oil, salt, pepper, and lemon juice. The fresh fruit, depending on the season, might be watermelon, cantaloupe, oranges, bananas, tangerines, or strawberries.

If guests were invited for lunch, extra food had to be prepared. Rather than a choice of either meat or chicken, both were served. Also, another vegetable, perhaps stuffed grape leaves, stuffed cabbage, or stuffed zucchini, was served, as well as more pastries. For example, ground beef–filled filo dough or such would be added to the menu when guests were present.

After lunch all members of the family took an afternoon siesta, which might last up to two hours. They woke up to a hot cup of tea and *baklava* or any similar dessert, such as *konafa* (similar to *baklava*, but made of shredded dough), cake, or cookies. Some people's work schedule called for working an evening session as well as the morning one. This usually started around 7:00 P.M. and lasted until 10:00 P.M. Dinner was always a very light meal. It might be yogurt, or a cheese sandwich, and it was served about 10:00 or 11:00 P.M.

All the meals described were served during the regular days of the year, but there were frequent exceptions to this style, when religious fasts with their special foods were to be observed. In the Coptic Christian religion, fasts were plenty; it seemed that hardly one fast was complete before the next one started. In addition, year round (except for the seven weeks after Resurrection), believers were not to eat dairy, meat, or seafood products on any Wednesday or Friday. On those days, legumes were eaten for protein. Vegetables and fruits became even more important during these weekly fasts. The same diet applied to the three-day fasts like the one in remembrance of the people of Nineveh, who some say fasted while Jonah was in the whale's belly. Longer fasts occurred during Lent, during the Apostle's fast (after the feast of the Ascension), for six weeks before Christmas (Christmas being January 7, according to the Coptic calendar), and for two weeks in August (in the name of Mary, the Mother of Jesus). During those times, the day started with total abstinence from food or drink for a number of hours, and the meals later were free of dairy products and meat. Some of the fasts allowed eating fish, some did not.

On the eve of the feast, whether it was Christmas or Easter, Christians went to church to attend Mass, which lasted until midnight. Then they'd go to their homes and eat a large meal before they went to sleep. That meal had to have meat and dairy products and a traditional main dish called *fatta*. There were different versions of *fatta*, but a standard one was pita bread cut into bite-size pieces and lightly fried, with chicken or beef broth poured over it, then white rice topped it on the platter, with bits of beef cut into stew-size pieces, cooked by boiling, and also lightly fried. Then a strong hot dressing was poured over the platter. That dressing was made of ground garlic fried in butter.

FASTS AND FEASTS

Help me with the chicken
And a beef slice.
One or the other will not suffice.
Pour the *molokhia* over my rice.
Serve the *fatta,*
Give me a large helping.
Today we are feasting.
Tomorrow, again we will abstain.
So go ahead and pile up my plate,
Before it's too late.

Muslims fast for a month, during which they do not eat or drink from sunrise to sunset. That month is called Ramadan. Their food choices after sunset are not limited, and the feast following that month is called Eid-el-Fitr. The feast is celebrated when the new moon is observed, and it is a three-day celebration. There is another feast during the year, no fast precedes that one; it is called Eid-el-Adha. They have to slaughter a lamb for sacrifice. Muslims too serve the *fatta* as an important traditional dish, and its meat topping is always from the lamb they sacrificed.

As Christians, but in America we tried to keep, and to get our children to keep, to Coptic traditions. Besides fasting as the Church requires us, we attended church regularly, and celebrated Christmas and Easter by attending prayers and eating traditional foods.

Our summer vacations were typically spent with the family overseas, sometimes with an extra stop, such as Switzerland or France for a three or four-day visit. This continued from the 1970s until the 1990s. Sometimes someone from my family would come to the United States to visit us, and it always made us feel good and special. The frequent visits with the families, both in Egypt and in England, helped us to stay close and to have our children keep in contact with the extended family in spite of the distance, the language, and the fact that we have three different nationalities within our family. Our children are Americans, born in the United States. My sister's children are Egyptians, born in Egypt. And my brother's children are British, born in England and raised there; also their mother, Anne, is British.

We never missed out on the opportunity to make this mixture of nationalities an entertaining matter. We would seat all six of the children for a meal, and address them by their nationality rather than by their names. So we would ask: "Brits, would you like some carrots?" or "Egyptians, would you like some chicken?" At a very young age, each one of them responded, knowing that he or she was the one addressed.

An incident that amused me a great deal was one summer in England when Nancy was four years old. We were at my sister's house, which was across the street from my brother's house. Anne's sister, Margaret, and her adult children and grandchildren were visiting. Aimie, the grandchild who was close in age to Nancy, came over and asked, "Would you skip with me?" Nancy asked Aimie to wait a minute. She came to me, told me what Aimie asked her, and said: "What does she want me to do?" I said, "She wants you to jump rope with her." It seemed very funny to me that I had to translate British English into American English, but Nancy's face lit up with the newly acquired knowledge and she left to skip with Aimie!

On that same trip we went to visit St. Paul's Cathedral, where earlier that year Prince Charles and Princess Diana were married. As a family we climbed the hundreds of narrow, winding steps. And so did Nancy, every one of them. When my sister told her British friends about our adventure, and that Nancy had climbed all the way to the highest level, they were surprised, and said they'd never heard of a child her age being able to do this. Isis cheerfully said, "Nancy broke a record!"

I looked at Nancy with a smile, only to find her face pale and her eyes filled with tears. She asked me, "What record did I break, Mom?" I laughed and explained to her the meaning of the expression.

Once again back home in the States after yet another vacation, I was asked to participate in several school activities such as bake sales, and helping teachers with activities with small groups of children. As our children got older, my involvement became more significant. For example, I helped with the Brownie troops, musical concerts, and in more academic subjects. When I was at that age, having parents just attend a school play was considered to be participation on their part. But I found myself devoted on a weekly basis to a schedule that was indeed involved. I did not realize that at that time, other mothers were too busy getting their careers started, which was why the help at school was short. For those parents who were able to offer help, the demand was intense. On occasion, the demand was more than I could keep up with. I felt I wanted to please everyone at home and at school. That was taking its toll on my patience:

> THE PLEASING ADDICTION
> I pleased them all.
> I ended up a corpse.
> I know you are pleased
> I am here to share with you
> Their every plea.
> Here comes the one
> With "please, please, please,"
> So I please.
> Then comes the opposing other
> With "please, please, please,"
> So I please.
> That is when the pleasing addiction
> Becomes a fatal contradiction.

In spite of how I felt sometimes about the excessive effort to help, I enjoyed the time with the children a great deal, and the highlight of it all was when I was asked by the third-grade teacher to make a presentation about my home country. They were studying that area of the world in their social studies class.

I wore my *galabia,* a long, loose, all-Egyptian cotton dress with designs embroidered all over. Then I packed a small suitcase with artifacts and went to the school to present Egypt and its culture to the class and their teachers. Afterward, other classes asked me for the same presentation. So did Alverno College in Milwaukee, which invited me to speak on one of their international dinner evenings, and I was delighted to oblige. It always gave me pleasure and satisfaction to talk about Egypt to Westerners.

PRESENTATION

They asked me to talk about you,
They want to know you better.
Joyfully I accepted,
Love's tongue I shall utter.
I bring up your name,
A magnitude of glory.
To talk about you is global,
Your past, present, or future,
Every heart you capture.
In the holy books you are mentioned,
In history books thereafter.
They call you "The gift of the Nile"
For the Nile ran down between,
And dressed Egypt in green.

I always took the children with me to Kohl's, the nearest grocery store, where we stocked up on food and daily needs. The cashiers knew us. They liked the children and were always playful and chatted with them. One morning, when the two children were at school, I went to the same grocery store. I had a few items, more than ten but not a cartful, either.

The store had switched the express checkout lane from the first to the second lane. Seeing that I had more than ten items, I went to the first cashier, the one that used to be for less than ten but was now open for more. I stood there, waiting for my turn, when an older, well-dressed man pushed my cart in an angry manner toward the other lane and attempted to take my place. The cashier in the express lane noticed and called out, "Express is here, sir." He quickly pushed his cart to that cashier and I pulled my cart back to place and started to unload it.

My mind silently worked on the situation that had just happened, thinking, *Just because I am a foreigner he wants to get me out of his way.*

At the same time, the cashier who knew me spoke out and said, "Men. Give them two of the many things that women can do at the same time and they can't handle it. They think we have nothing to do."

My silent thoughts came to a screeching halt when they collided head-on with the cashier's voiced words. While I had been thinking race, she had been thinking gender. How many misunderstandings happen all the time, everywhere in this world? In my situation, it could have been both, either, or neither reason. After all, maybe the man had an appointment to keep and this was the unfortunate way he'd reacted.

Most immigrants to the United States group together by country of origin, and the Egyptians in Chicago were no different. In the early eighties, a traditional Coptic church was built from the ground up to replace the previous one, which had been bought already built. The old church did not comply with the traditional Coptic Orthodox rites, which call for, among other things, the altar to be facing east. This is for several reasons. Jesus Christ, who is the True Light and the Sun of Righteousness, was born in the East, and the star announcing His birth shone in that same direction. He also ascended in the East, as was witnessed by His disciples. Another reason why Coptic Christians face the East when they pray is to be reminded of the lost paradise, and of the Lord's anticipated second coming, spoken of to the disciples by an angel.

A Coptic church must also have twelve pillars, representing the twelve disciples who spread Christianity all over the world. In addition to this, more details regarding what may or may not appear in the icons are also dictated by the Church's rites. For example, in the Last Supper painting, when the disciples are feasting on the Passover meal, all twelve are to appear seated at the table. If, however, the painting shows Jesus breaking the bread and the wine after the feast, symbolic of our communion today, then only eleven disciples should appear because, according to the Bible, Judas Iscariot left to betray Jesus and therefore did not participate in taking communion.

Such details were all present in our newly built church, and it made us a very proud group of Egyptian Christians in Chicago. In the early eighties, the church was ready for the congregation to attend Mass, and along with the many friends we made there, we enjoyed Christmas, Easter, and all the traditional celebrations throughout the year.

In the meantime, the Egyptian Christian community in Milwaukee was also growing, but at a slower pace. The group was finally able to buy a church in 1990. Named St. Mary and St.

Antonious Church, it was in Waterford, Wisconsin. For the first few years the priest from Chicago would come every other Saturday to conduct Mass for our Milwaukee congregation. Then, in 1993, Pope Shenouda III assigned Father Rewis Awadalla to come from Egypt and serve as the priest in the parish of St. Mary and St. Antonious.

It was during this same time, in the early 1990s, when we realized that all our nieces and nephews were growing up, for news of their weddings started to be sent our way. One very dear wedding that I was unable to attend was Moni's to his bride, Hoda. The timing did not work for us. The only way we were able to participate was by telephone, which was becoming our means of intra-family communication rather than letters, largely due to overseas telephone-system improvements made around a political event.

In June 1975 the American president, Mr. Nixon, visited the Middle East. Egypt was a very important destination for him, since it is regarded as the oldest sister of all the countries in the area. His visit with Egyptian President Anwar el-Sadat, who had assumed office after the death of President Nasser in 1970, was the first to Egypt by an American president. The prospect of peace for Egypt was felt very strongly that year, due to a peace treaty signed with Israel the previous fall, to this visit, and to the reopening of the Suez Canal.

It was the age of computers, of communication satellites, and therefore of instant live TV broadcasts and of better-quality overseas phone connections. The media stretched its muscle for Nixon's visit and went to the Egyptian desert to plant the most up-to-date equipment in the belly of the Land of Pharaoh.

We watched Mr. Nixon and Mr. Sadat on live TV as if the two hemispheres had become one. The delight of every Egyptian American went way beyond the political scene. No longer did the thousands of us need an operator to put the call through. No longer did we speak over a line clouded with static. We now dialed trans-Atlantic calls directly, and the lines were clear, as if we were talking to our next-door neighbor. In the midst of this instant gratification, we almost forgot the "ancient art" of letter writing: We simply dialed, heard the voices of loved ones, had our questions answered, and finalized plans without waiting for the mail, which could take weeks or even months.

* * *

As for my personal career, I had continued to do my volunteer work at school until the mid-1980s when I felt that my children were almost grown up. When Carmen was approaching her teens and Nancy starting to be more independent at age nine, I switched my volunteer work from school to the public library, to refresh what I had learned in Hartford. But that was not all I wanted to do. I wanted to go back to the world of business.

I went to a job-search agency for help, and found that while I had been busy raising the children and helping with the school field trips, bake sales, and brownies, the computer had invaded the business world. I was a stranger to this new corporate world, and it was just as foreign to me. I felt like a Rip Van Winkle of the late twentieth century. The harsh facts were given to me by the employment agency staff. Unless I went to school and learned how to use a computer, I was not an employable person.

A feeling of uselessness and hopelessness shrouded my every sense. I could not find my way to the door to let myself out of the agency in order to take a deep breath of fresh air, to possibly revive my senses so that I could drive back home, to start once again thinking about what I should do with myself for the rest of my life.

NOW THEY E-MAIL THEM

I sent in my application:
In speedwriting I take dictation.
After the punctuation,
I type them, fold them, and I stuff them.
Then I seal them, stamp them, and mail them.

Oh! But now they e-mail them!
"Your skill has long expired.
Your boss has since retired.
Come back when you've updated
Your knowledge, which is now outdated."

After intense consideration, I thought that since I loved traveling and I had a lot of personal experience with it, if I put that knowledge together with the computer courses, I could find my way in the world of travel.

For the next eleven weeks I attended a comprehensive travel course, which was held six days a week, all day. On Saturdays I took a computer course. And from Monday through Friday I studied other aspects of travel management. This effort to reattach myself to the outside world culminated successfully with the completion of both courses.

After graduation I took a job as an outside sales agent for a travel agency, owned by three very kind women. They helped me learn, practice, and grow. My clients started as a very small group, and grew constantly. Friends told their friends, and my children grew up and went to college and their friends purchased their tickets from me.

Changes happened in the business. Offices were moved and agencies sold, but I continued with the same type of work I'd done when I started.

As the years progressed, the family members grew up. In 1991 Carmen graduated from high school and was to start her college education in the fall at Northwestern University in Evanston, Illinois. The following summer, soon after Moni and Hoda's wedding in Egypt, Mark and Anne announced that they were getting married. The wedding was to take place in England. We were fortunate enough to be able to attend their beautiful wedding and to experience British wedding traditions, as opposed to Egyptian and American wedding traditions. For the first time in my life I wore a hat in such a formal manner.

Mary Therese came to visit me with Alaa, her fiancé, in the summer of 1993. I was so happy to receive them; we had a great time together. I wanted to promise them that I would go to Egypt to attend their wedding but could not do that, as I was not sure I would be able to keep my word. It was a good thing I didn't promise, because they set their wedding day at a time when I was unable to be there. Soon after, I was able to visit Egypt and to see their new home.

Once again, in May of 1995, there was a wedding and I was unable to attend. Nadia, my niece, and John were married in

England. We were lucky to be able to go and see them after they returned to England from their exotic honeymoon. First they went to France, then to the French and British Caribbean, St. Maarten and St. Thomas.

That was the same year that Carmen graduated from Northwestern University and Nancy graduated from high school, ready to start college that fall. A funny incident happened when I was attending an informational meeting in Milwaukee about Loyola University, which is in Chicago. After the representative from Loyola was done talking to the parents, we decided to drive to Chicago to see the school but were not sure how to get there. I asked him, "Which exit do we take to get to Loyola?" He answered promptly, saying, "Touhy." The word *too-hy* in Arabic means "get lost." I felt insulted for a split second, thinking, "Here I am ready to send my daughter to receive her higher education at his school and this is the kind of answer I get!" But I quickly remembered driving on the expressway and reading the name of that exit. The young man probably thought I was mapping the area in my mind. Nancy did finally attend Loyola.

Our enthusiasm for travel has never faded. We always wanted to get together and to see all the new family members and the older ones too. We wanted to be active members of the family as much as possible. We wished to see Moni and Hoda's baby, Carol; and Mark and Anne's baby, Alexander. This was a difficult undertaking, because of busy schedules and expenses.

As usual we were always making the effort, especially when there was yet another baby to see, Nadeem, Mary Therese and Alaa's little baby boy.

This thought of wanting to be with all the family, and being unable to, left me feeling short of strength and of the rejuvenating energy that comes only from being with extended family and close friends. But I found that I could recharge some of this energy by going to listen to the poets read their writings at a nearby café. The Espresso Poetry Evenings were a great source of strength and an alternative to my reading the classics aloud to myself, a practice I had enjoyed for years.

After listening to the poets at the café I started to put my thoughts on paper and write more of my own poems. This is how I started:

IN SEARCH OF STRENGTH
>   I will dance and sing
>   I will flap my wings
>   I will climb and scale
>   I will dive and swim
>   I will fly to France
>   I will love and hate
>   I will meet my fate
>   I will look ahead
>   I will fix my state
>   I WILL WRITE POETRY.

Talking about family and the strength one draws from close members reminds me of my childhood, particularly of the 1956 war, when everyone cuddled together to try and cope with the tough experience of every war day.

6

Life in Egypt under Nasser

It was very important to my parents that we live close to our school—English Mission College, in Qubba Palace, a suburb northeast of Cairo—so that they would be on hand in case of any emergency. (The suburb is so named because it is in the neighborhood of one of King Farouk's many palaces.) This never proved more important than that one afternoon in October 1956, when toward the end of the day Miss Hicks, our Canadian headmistress, walked into our classroom while we were packing our schoolbags to go home and said, "I want you to take home as many books as you can carry, and tomorrow morning, if your parents tell you to go to school, you come; if they ask you to stay at home, do whatever they say you should do."

I thought to myself, *With my luck, my parents wouldn't ever let me stay home.*

I did what she said and carried home as many books as I could. When the bell rang, announcing the end of the school day, we walked out of the classroom. Some students were picked up by their chauffeur-driven family cars; others rode the elegant brown-and-beige (our school colors) buses. There were ten of these buses owned by the school, and they picked up and dropped off students throughout Cairo and its suburbs. That afternoon we joked about whose parents would let them come to school the next day and whose would not. Since I lived around the corner from school, I walked home as usual.

I heard a couple of loud explosions as I was walking, but our neighborhood was so close to the military academy that we were used to hearing the sounds of war. We were also close to the military airport and were used to the loud sounds of their airplanes when they took off and landed. The explosions were, unbeknownst to me, two bombs. They were just a bit louder and stronger than what I was apt to hear regularly so, in my ignorance, I continued walking, unconcerned, until I reached home.

I looked up, toward our balcony on the third floor from the street, and saw my father, my mother, and my sister Samia waiting for my arrival. Such attention made me feel great—but I wondered what it was for. Was this some special occasion?

I walked up the three floors and there they were again, all three of them, meeting me by the staircase. Mother looked very nervous, and Father's smile was definitely hiding something. My sister looked both curious and relieved. For a moment we all stood there in silence, each waiting for someone else to say something first.

Then, in a tremulous voice, Mother asked me, "Hmm? Did you hear anything? Did they tell you anything at school?" I was wondering why everyone was so anxious. It was just the end of another school day, wasn't it? Aloud, I told mother, "Nothing." She persisted. "Nothing at all?"

I hesitated. Then I said, "Well, I heard a couple of military training bombs; they were stronger than the usual ones. And Miss Hicks told us to take home as many books as we could carry. She also said that if our parents tell us not to go to school tomorrow, then we should stay at home, but if they tell us to go to school, then we should go. She told us to do whatever our parents tell us."

My father decided to help Mother break the news to me, which they probably thought would scare me to death. Smiling, he said, "It's a war." *War,* I said to myself. *So now that it's war, what do we do?* Sometimes it's a blessing not to understand the seriousness of a situation. It did not scare me until nighttime, when the lights had to stay out even though it wasn't bedtime yet. There was nothing for us to do other than to sit in the dark, scared, and pray. We listened to the news when that was possible, and just wished that the war would end. This war was brought on by Nasser, the Egyptian leader, nationalizing the Suez Canal—a deed that got Britain, France, and Israel so angry that they attacked Egypt.

Nasser was a military man with great ambition and a brilliant mind. He wanted Egypt to become free and self-ruling after its decades of being colonized by the French, then by the British. He wanted to give back to the Egyptian people their sovereignty and their land.

He formed a group named The Free Officers, and planned to get the British completely out of Egypt.

In the past, Egypt had been ruled by the Arabs (from 641 A.D. to 1517) and then by the Turks, during the Ottoman Empire. Napoléon's armies occupied Egypt from 1798 until 1801. In 1805 Mohammed Ali was selected by the Turkish sultan, the head of the Ottoman Empire, to be pasha, the ranking head of Egypt. The Suez Canal, completed in 1869, though begun by both the French and the British under Turkish rule, increasingly came into British power. By the time of King Fouad, in 1914, Egypt had officially become a British protectorate, leaving Turkey with no further claims. All the canal's income, therefore, went to Britain, who no longer had to pay transport taxes for all the goods they brought to and from the Far East through the canal. By the 1950s, under King Farouk, Egypt was officially an independent country, but Britain still owned all rights to the canal.

The army, led by General Mohammed Naguib and The Free Officers, seized power on July 23, 1952. The coup took place in Alexandria, where the king was at the time, at the Ras-el-Tin palace. A few days later, at 6.00 A.M. on July 26, 1952, King Farouk abdicated in favor of his infant son and left by the end of the day. But the abdication was a formality only. In June 1953 the monarchy was formally abolished and a republic proclaimed, mainly ruled by the military junta. In 1954, Nasser took over the power of the junta and was proclaimed president.

Gamal Abdel Nasser proceeded to nationalize the Suez Canal. The British were very much disturbed because this meant that their path to the Far East, which was their economic livelihood, was falling out of their control. Nasser did not try to allay British fears. As a result, Britain first withdrew financial support of such ambitious projects as the Aswān High Dam, in the hope of holding on to ownership of at least some of Egypt's wealth. When this didn't work, along with France, Britain attacked Egypt in October 1956.

The two European powers then asked Israel to join them. The three nations descended upon Egypt with all their military power. The fighting was mainly by the Red Sea, east of Cairo. However, there were frequent air raids in the capital to destroy the airports, the military school, and military headquarters, close to our home.

America, though an ally of Britain and France, did not see any reason for the war. It did not join its allies.

With England and France—its normal allies—attacking it, Egypt turned to the then Soviet Union (USSR) for help, asking it to send out word that the attackers should stop. The Soviet Union announced that if this attack did not come to a quick end, it would have to defend Egypt.

The Soviet Union's threat brought action. For since the USSR would be defending against NATO countries, America would have had to join the war to stand by its allies. The translation of which would have been World War III. No one wanted this to happen.

American President Dwight D. Eisenhower and other U.N. countries formally warned the aggressors, and nine days after Britain's attack on Egypt, a cease-fire took place. After a lot of negotiations, a treaty was signed that provided for a U.N. peacekeeping force to patrol the Suez Canal and keep it open. (But though the canal ended up being Egypt's free and clear, parts of the Sinai did not, until June 1975, the time of American President Nixon's visit to Egypt.)

Despite the war, Nasser did so much to give Egypt a boost, economically and in terms of self-rule, that he was a great hero in his people's eyes. He had gotten rid of the king and his corrupt lifestyle, then he had taken giant steps toward reclaiming ownership of a major Egyptian asset: the Suez Canal. He stood firm against the attackers, three strong powers, making them respect the nationhood of Egypt, and his negotiations with the Soviet Union had brought peace back to the land.

During his term of office, he tried hard to win the love of the rural population by promising farmers five acres of land each. This would allow them to enjoy the feeling of working for themselves, a change from being servants to the landlords who had owned it. Nasser did this by nationalizing land owned by foreigners, taking possession of it in the name of Egypt, then it was distributed to Egyptian farmers.

Nasser went even further. He felt that enough was enough for the wealthy. He sequestered their business establishments and everything they owned, whether they were foreign or Egyptian. Heart attacks and instant deaths were common happenings in Egypt in that time, for there was nowhere for such families to turn to complain. Once authorities sealed the place and put the guards at the doors, it became federal property. The owners had no recourse but to comply. It seemed that Nasser thought of himself as a Robin Hood—he took from the rich to give to the poor.

He then started to build the Aswān High Dam, the birth of industrial Egypt to alleviate the poverty caused by war and his effort to isolate Egypt. In his speeches he told the Egyptian public that they would become self-sufficient, there would be nothing the country would need to import from the West; in fact it would be Egypt who would export what the West needed.

Nasser was charismatic, a father figure, strong-willed, and industrious. When he appeared on television his voice sent a serene message to his people and he had all their attention, and their trust in his power.

LEADER

Nasser, we loved you;
Sometimes we did not.
Self-sufficiency, you called for,
Not at all an easy goal.
We stood in long lines
For necessities so rare,
We envied the countries
With oodles to spare.
Feta cheese we had to eat,

Because cheddar was not there.
You triggered the wars.
Fighting gave way to fear,
Fear gave birth to hatred
But you were always so dear.
Charisma you had, and ambition too.
The inhabitants of Egypt
Were at a geometrical swell.
The strip by the Nile
Was about to explode.
You built the High Dam,
"Another pyramid," we thought.
"Industry," you said,
"Will feed the population."
But then you died,
Leaving us to meet our destiny.

During the nine days of the October 1956 war we needed shelter. We lived in a strategic area, very near the center of military power, so the steady and heavy bombings were close by. We found that the best place to be during air raids was low to the ground—or better yet, underground. We'd had no notice to arrange such a place, so the nearest shelter was downstairs, in our first-floor neighbor's apartment. They opened their home to the whole building. We would all gather there during air raids, in the dark required for safety, using only candles for light behind the heavy shutters.

One of the neighbors had a large family and the grandmother lived with them, too. The old lady was so worried about every member in her family that every few minutes she would call the roll. She would start by calling her son, then his wife, then the children in the order of their birth. Each one had to answer "here, Grandma!" By the end of the roll call, it would be time for her to start again. This amused us. My sister and I tried to keep our laughter down to a smile, as they could not see us smile in the dark.

When the siren announced the end of an air raid, we would go back upstairs to our own apartments. It seemed that we'd just get ready to sleep when the next air raid would begin, and the whole routine started once again.

One time when my mother was closing the shutters in my room so that I could go to sleep, she saw bright lights in the sky. She called out, "The war is over." My father came quickly and asked, "How do you know that?" She said, "Look at the fireworks. They are celebrating." "Celebrating!" he exclaimed. "That is the enemy lighting the city to see where to hit. Get the children out of bed and let's run downstairs."

This is bitter, I grumbled into my pillow, feeling that disturbing my sleep was a cruel thing to do. *How can they do this to me? I'd rather the whole building collapse! Do I have to get out of bed again?*

Our good neighbor with the large family and the grandmother, Mr. Girgis, was a respectable schoolteacher. He had been teaching geography at the English Mission College for years, and acted as school principal whenever the British principal had to go to England for business or on a personal trip.

After the first night of spending air raids on the first floor of our apartment building, Mr. Girgis got the school key, and for three nights his family and ours would go to the basement of English Mission College. We'd bring the gym mattresses and cover the floor with them, and we would sit down on them and talk, then go to sleep. The good thing about the basement was that it had no windows, so we could put the lights on and have the place lit without disturbing the darkness that had to cover the whole country every evening. It was a very strange feeling being at school but not attending classes; also being there at night and then going home during the day. It seemed as if we were living in reverse order; our emotions were a mixture of fear and apprehension.

Because my father's job was a civilian job in the heart of the bomb zone, he could not go to work. So he stayed home with us.

My brother had graduated in May of that year from medical school and he was training as resident at a nearby hospital. All doctors were on alert for emergency services, so Samir was not permitted to leave the hospital to go home. After a day or so, Mother was sure he'd be needing some of his items from home, and she felt she had no choice but to send them to him with my sister, Samia. Needless to say, it would be very dangerous for her to be on the streets. It seemed to me that my mother was in a situation similar to that of Abraham taking Isaac, his son, to sacrifice him: I thought she was sacrificing Samia to help Samir.

Samia did not seem to mind the thought of going, but I was sitting back there grinding my teeth, burning my brain over what would be the best thing to do. Mother was hesitating, pacing the apartment, when we heard a knock at the door. It was my brother. What a relief for everyone! He had been given a couple of free hours to rest, so he had come home. That must have seemed to my mother like the time God furnished the lamb for sacrifice and spared Isaac.

Several more tense moments filled the hours of those days. One day a neighbor came over and announced to Mother that the enemy had hit all the hospitals in the country; not one had been spared. This piece of news was harsh; it took a while to clear it up and find the facts. We were very grateful that it was not exactly "all" the hospitals, although there were many that were hit. Some hospitals along the eastern border were hit really hard, but the one where my brother worked was in the city, and had been spared.

The war continued, and the family we spent the nights with in the school basement decided to leave the city and go to their relatives in the countryside. They offered us the key to the school basement, but we did not feel that we wanted to be there anymore. We too needed company and family. We packed, as my father advised, and we went to my uncle's house, the home where my maternal grandparents spent the final years of their lives.

Uncle Aziz and his family welcomed us and were happy to see that we had made the decision to stay with them rather than continue to live in that northeast suburb of Heliopolis. My uncle's youngest daughter, Salwa, was a baby. It amazed me so much to watch her so peaceful. She slept and woke up, following her own little schedule, undisturbed by bombs, darkness, or the lack of peace that we experienced.

At my uncle's home, we also had the opportunity to see my aunt and her family, because they lived nearby. Also, my other uncle, Selim, and more cousins and friends. We visited, talked, played, and even laughed when we could get a bit of cheer in.

It seemed to me that it was a long war. The headmistress's words would ring a bell in my head every now and then.

I finally understood what she meant when she said, "Do whatever your parents say." If only I hadn't listened to her and brought home all the books I could carry! I wouldn't have had to study during the day, and who knows, maybe the school would be bombed and I wouldn't have to go back to school! Then all that studying would be for nothing! Wishful thinking of a fifth grader!

But it is not only little people who imagine and wish this way. One day, when we were indoors, we heard loud shouting. When we looked down from the balcony, there was a large group of youth from the area, those who were not old enough to go to the front lines. They were carrying a live-size coffin, and walking down the street chanting:

> "Eden mat ya Gamal
> Dafanna fil Kanal!"

which translated:

> "Eden died, Gamal, [Nasser's first name]
> We buried him in the Canal." [Suez Canal]

I believed that Eden, the British Prime Minister, was dead and that he was in the coffin, but I wondered why this was the group of people who had taken over the responsibility of burying him.

My mother explained to me that when people wish so hard for something, their power for make-believe takes over, and it can result in an imaginary scene such as the one we were watching. I thought they must have been feeling about Eden (the enemy) as I had been feeling about studying.

I was very bored since none of my friends lived in the neighborhood, and the war days seemed endless. I missed playing hopscotch, as this was my favorite game during break time at school. We would draw the lines in the sand and find a nice flat rock to kick with one foot while hopping with the other one off the ground, its knee bent backward. I also missed jumping rope, and gathering as a group of girls to watch the boys being rough and active playing their favorite game, The Fight. They would divide their group into two teams and start playing, or rather, fighting. They would invite us to watch as they pulled each other down to the ground and start hitting and kicking. We would express our distaste for such behavior among ourselves, but when The Fight was over, we would congratulate and encourage them. Was this out of fear, since we had just observed what they are capable of doing, or out of caring for their egos, in an example of our developing the expected cultural roles of the sexes? A question for psychologists to answer.

When it was finally announced that the war was over and life could return back to normal, we returned to our home. Things at home were just the same as when we left them, but when we went to school, they were quite different. The fact that England had been the aggressor was obvious even to us children.

The name of the school, which had been English Mission College, was changed to Al-Salam College, meaning the School of Peace. The British staff (Miss Lomas, Miss Hicks, Mr. Butcher, Miss Westlake, and others) had left the country and were replaced by an Egyptian staff. These were graduates from the same school; they had gotten their degrees in education and returned to teach there.

Mr. Girgis became the school headmaster and Mrs. Helmy, the school headmistress. She was a graduate of the school who had gone on to receive her degree in education in England. I had no doubt that these people put in a great effort to run the school the way it originally had been.

More changes came gradually. Instead of a Saturday and Sunday weekend (Christian and Jewish sabbaths), we had to have Friday and Sunday (Moslem and Christian sabbaths). Another change was that we no longer had to attend the morning assembly where, after the morning bell rang, we would go first to our classrooms, unpack our books, line up behind our classroom teacher, and go to the assembly hall for a morning prayer, Bible reading, hymn singing, and to listen to the day's announcements delivered by the school headmistress or one of the teachers. This procedure was replaced by going to the courtyard, where we stood surrounding the Egyptian flag, saluted it, sang a national song, then we would go to our classrooms to resume our daily school programs. We did not like any of the changes.

Military training courses were introduced at the school, for students in the final three years. When we entered the Upper

Four (tenth grade) we would be taught the military training course by a military female teacher. She brought in (of all makes!) a British gun, and talked to us about the reasons why we had to take this course. She was dressed in her military uniform, and in her deep voice, she taught us in Arabic that we would have to defend ourselves and our younger sisters and brothers, as well as our grandparents, in case of another war.

When I got to that level in school, four years after the war, I tried to excuse myself from the course, saying that I was the youngest in the family and both sets of grandparents were dead. But that did not excuse me from having to carry the gun and learn to load it with ammunition. This filled me with a feeling of hatred mixed with curiosity. The only thing I was able to accept was learning the rules for shooting.

My uncle Selim loved hunting, and he was a military engineer. It always amazed me how he aimed and hit the target regardless of distance or motion. The military training course gave me the opportunity to learn and to experience the technique of shooting. In fact, I ended up being a member of the shooting club, and every day I spent part of my lunch break in the woods behind the school's main playground, practicing with the club.

I accepted the military course just so I would graduate. We were told that if we didn't pass this military training course, we would not be permitted to sit for our final exams.

After the 1956 war, my sister Isis left Egypt for England. She had graduated from medical school, and she left to accompany her husband, who was a physician and had gone to England for his continuing education. This experience was so hard for me. Her leaving Egypt for England felt to me like the end of the world. Then my brother, Samir, left for Sudan. The family of six had shrunk to four, leaving a vacuum in our lives. We had only writing letters for keeping in touch. After two years, Samir left Sudan, visited us in Egypt briefly, and went on to England. We learned from him that his two years had been filled with adventures. Once, hearing a knock at the door and looking out to see who was there, he saw a snake. He brought a flashlight and directed its beam toward the snake's eyes, which made it move away.

As for me and my sister Samia, we developed a closer relationship during those years. We went out together to the movies, to picnics, and visiting friends and cousins. We just enjoyed ourselves. I was not excluded from her group of friends even though they were older than I. They used to attend evening classes, then they would stop at our home for a chat, since we were so close to the school. We had a little arrangement. One of them would pay for a treat each time they were to come—perhaps a special kind of chewy candy that took a long time to eat! Since they were grown-ups and did not want to go to the store to buy candy like little children do, I was brought into the picture. That was where I benefited from the deal! The one whose turn it was to pay for the candy would hand me the money before class, and I would buy the candy for all the group and include myself. This was how they paid me for the service, and I enjoyed it as well as the company of the older girls.

Samia often fascinated me with her knowledge of English literature by reciting a list of the names of poets and authors, which seemed endless, and the most musical and amusing poems, any time of the day or night. One day while she was at school and I was home reading a book of poems, I came across one that I liked very much. I looked to see the name of the poet and it was signed "Anonymous." It was a capital *A,* indicating a proper noun. I thought, *Here is a poet Samia's never mentioned; I am going to test her on it.* I marked the page, and when she came home, I pulled out the book and asked her to listen to me. I took a deep breath and started reading the poem. To my satisfaction, she did not know the poem or who wrote it. Proud as a peacock, and in a mocking tone, I asked her, "Do you know the poet Anonymous?" She held back a smile, which I thought was meaningless at the time, and said, "Yes, he wrote some of the best poems in English literature." She started to name some of them, then to recite them to me. I was very disappointed by that and said, "So you do know Anonymous!" At this she burst out with laughter and told me, "Don't tell me you don't know what anonymous means!" I was so embarrassed when she finally explained to me the meaning of the word!

On another occasion, Samia and I were ready to go out and we were trying to keep an appointment. We were at the door, ready to leave, when she said, "Wait a minute, Mary." She ran to her room. I waited by the door, thinking that she'd just gone back to pick up a jacket or something. After a long wait I went to check on her. When I walked into her room I found her standing by her desk with a poetry book in her hand, reading away. I got upset, but she explained to me that she had been reciting a poem in her mind and she'd forgotten a line. Had we left without checking that line, she would have had a very miserable outing.

Samia also loved dogs. Uncle Selim, who loved all kinds of animals and birds, as well as motorcycles and cars, gave Samia a puppy. The dog's name was Katy. She was the sweetest puppy I have ever seen: a fox terrier with the most perfect distribution of black dots on her white body, and the shortest tail ever—in fact, hardly any tail at all. She was playful, happy, loving, and very active.

Katy was loved by everyone in the family or anyone who saw her. One day I left the house to run a few errands. She followed me. I did not have her leash, so I went along making my stops, and after one of them I turned around to call her. She had disappeared. The long search started, but the dog was nowhere to be found. Someone must have stolen her because she would have come back home had she been able to. We felt as though we had lost a member of our family. I never forgot her, and I feel guilty to this day that I did not get her leash when I found that she was following me.

Uncle Selim tried to replace her by giving Samia Katy's brother, Jerry. But Jerry was epileptic. When he was healthy, he was as good as Katy had been, but when he was sick, he was in a very bad condition. One day he went to the veterinarian's. We children were told he would be cared for, but he never came back home. We were left to figure out what we could from that—that he had been put to sleep, or not.

Not only was Samia a literature fan and a dog lover, but she was also an athlete. At school, she was the house games captain. She always encouraged me to participate in sports and in the sports day held annually by our school, to compete against its two sister schools. Samia, of course, participated in most of the sports, such as the obstacle race, the high jump, the broad jump (this was for girls only—the equivalent to the boys' long jump), and netball (the girls' equivalent to boys' basketball).

I always acted as though I were listening to her tips and advice, then I would do the exact opposite. She used to tell me not to look behind me while running a race but to keep my eyes aimed straight ahead. Also, not to think about the competitors. During practice, I'd look behind me every now and then so that I would slow down and not qualify for the race on the big day.

The school sports I mentioned here are the ones our school offered us at the time, but the main sport activity enjoyed by the whole country was soccer. It was popular everywhere and Egypt had many different teams. The two most famous, the ones everyone looked forward to seeing play, were the teams that belonged to the two most famous private clubs in Egypt. They were both in Cairo: the Ahly, and the Zamalek. Families gathered around the TV Friday afternoons to watch them play.

When Samia graduated from college, she applied for jobs at a number of places. One day she was going for a translation test for a job with one of the journals. The night before her test, she asked me to buy her the English newspaper, the *Gazette* when I went out with my friends for a walk that evening. She wanted to refresh her memory of journalistic idioms. I was more than willing to do this for her, but the newsstands were out of the *Gazette;* they only had some French and Arabic newspapers left. We did not give up. We continued walking and searching. When we got to the farthest one, I saw at a glance the pile of the Arabic paper, *Al-Ahram,* and on the other end the French paper. There was a pile in the middle. Since English, French, and Arabic were the three languages commonly used, I felt I did not even have to check it. I picked up a copy from the middle pile and paid the newspaper vendor, then rushed back home.

Samia met me at the door. I handed her the paper and said, "Here you are, we had to go to the end of the world to find it because it was so late in the day." Then I started walking toward my room. I heard a loud bang. I turned around to see what had happened. There was Samia on the floor. I rushed to help her, but she was laughing so hard she couldn't catch her breath. "Look at the paper," she gasped while rolling on the floor. I looked, and I found that it was a *Greek* paper! I started to laugh too.

My parents came to ask us what was going on. When they found out the reason, my father turned to me and said teasingly,

"Eleven years at an English school and you can't tell English from Greek?"

Those were four of the best years of my life. Samia then got a job with the Sudanese airline. Within a year she met a young man, Nabil, who was working for British Airways (at the time it was called British Overseas Airways Corporation, or BOAC), and they got married. It was very hard to let Samia leave home too, especially since this left me an "only child."

7
Teenage Years and Father's Death

After the 1956 war and until it was time for me to graduate from high school I was concentrating on receiving my education and growing with a group of my friends. In my classroom, there were two other Marys. We enjoyed each other's company, as the same name seemed to bring us closer. One of our tricks was to sit very close to each other in a triangular setting so that when the teacher would call "Mary," the one of us who knew the right answer would stand up very quickly and say it. It did not take our teachers too long to figure out our little plan and to separate us, each in a different corner of the classroom. Our friendship continued and our little tricks were played on members of our families often.

One of the Marys liked to ask me to go with her to all her activities. She introduced me to the YWCA in Cairo. We would go there and watch educational films and learn different arts, including sewing. We also went together to march in military shows presented by the schools. I was never really eager to go to any of the marches, but she used to come and pick me up. She would bring me a clean, pressed uniform so that I would not have an excuse to not go along.

The one thing I am most grateful to this Mary for, even today, is the way she insisted on making me volunteer at the school library. When she asked me to go and help, I felt that I was sacrificing my fun time to help the librarian take inventory. I thought, *Why should I spend my break in the library with books?* Mary, however, was a good friend, very convincing and ambitious, so I went along. The library was all cupboards with glass doors, and the shelves inside each cupboard held the books, in alphabetical order by topic.

I was asked to work on one cupboard when the title of a book—*Beethoven*—caught my eye. *The great musician,* I thought. I glanced at the pages and went on with my work, saying to myself, *Next time I'm here to borrow books I will take this book and read a great person's biography!* That was the first time I enjoyed and appreciated reading for pleasure in my young life. The ups and downs in that man's life were very touching: his poverty, his temper, his art, and his deafness. I cried and I laughed, I heard music and bursts of temper in the pages of his life. I returned the book after reading it, only to borrow another one from that same section. This time it was Schubert. When Schubert heard a tune in his head, he had to write it down instantly, the author said. When no paper was around, he grabbed anything to write on, he would even cover the tablecloth with his compositions!

I was convinced by then that books could be a source of joy. No longer heavy awkward objects to me, I now saw them as handy containers; dispensers of exciting adventures, knowledge, and true experiences; vast goblets of fascinating information and amusement.

I made a vow to myself that if I ever had the chance to see where any of the composers lived, I would make a point of going there to learn more about them. Composers fascinated me.

Many years later, in 1981, I had the opportunity to visit Vienna with my family. We asked the tour guide, "Where did Beethoven live?" We were surprised at his reaction and that of the other tour guides. They didn't seem to care much about the composer.

"He lived in many places," one said to us. "He had to leave because he was poor and didn't pay the rent. So the landlords would throw him out." Another said, "He had a bad temper because he could not hear his compositions due to his deafness."

None of Beethoven's homes were marked by the Austrian flag, as was the tradition there. All the homes of the other composers and important personalities have the Austrian flag flying to identify the place as a landmark.

I found that Johann Strauss, sometimes called the Waltz King, was their number one composer. I remember reading his biography too, but it was not as clear in my mind as that of Beethoven. I learned more about Strauss, and saw his statues in parks and public places all over Vienna. We were also told that he used to have his own concerts at age six, and that he was tutored by his father, Johann Baptiste Strauss.

Our school system required us to make a choice for our future at the beginning of the last three years in high school. We had to let them know whether we were going to take our courses in science, arts, or economics. Looking back at my childhood, I think I was very lucky, since I was familiar with the first two areas of study.

I had my sister Isis and my brother, Samir, in the sciences and my sister Samia in the arts. I remembered how, when they baby-sat me now and then when Mother was out visiting or whatever, Isis had to examine each and every slide under the microscope, and I insisted she let me look before she removed it. I would look at the colors and shapes of bacteria; they amused me. I remembered watching Isis dissect a frog (*after* lunch) several times. I praised her expertise in cutting the skin and not damaging the heart when it was obviously throbbing. Isis and Samir had human skeletons at home, and depending on the day, they would either explain the parts to me or try to playfully scare me with them!

When I got really bored and wanted Mother back, I would cry. Then Samir would sing me a song in his deep voice: "Oh Susannah, don't you cry for me..." I was young, and thought he didn't even know my name. Then he would follow the song with a show of the latest pieces of medical equipment he had purchased; perhaps a penlight and tiny mirror for checking the ear, nose, and throat. So, despite my youthful misunderstanding sometimes, the biological sciences were familiar to me when it came time to choose my field of concentration.

Samia, on the other hand, would tell me stories such as that of King Lear and his three daughters, how two were so unkind to him that he felt that, in his words, "My punishment is greater than my sin." I was very touched by his sadness, but I wished the names of his daughters were a little easier so that I could tell my friends the story. I didn't know yet that I was listening to a famous Shakespearean play, only that the story was moving.

Also, the story of the little orphan boy, David. Charles Dickens's *David Copperfield* is still my favorite novel. I hoped I would never have to experience what happened to him. It would be hard to have to go away from home to attend school under the supervision of such seemingly tough people. The ghosts and witches, the poor and the rich, all the characters of the stories Samia told me about were more colorful than the slides Isis showed me or the bright light Samir had let me try to use.

So I told my parents I wanted to study literature. Mother was eager for me to do more than that. To please her, I looked into taking economics. I found out that if I took economics, I could also take literature along with it; this seemed to be the ideal choice, since I could find out about it without risking losing my chance to continue with the arts. Not all the courses were interesting because I had to take bookkeeping and shorthand, and I didn't care for those two.

During summer vacation in 1960 there was a military training camp for girls in Port Said, the area that was torn apart by the 1956 war. The city by then had started to rebuild. My friend Mary convinced me to join the camp. Many other friends had advised me not to go. They said, "It's not going to be a happy experience." I went anyway. I said to myself, *It's a girl's summer camp, not a real military camp.*

Once I got there, I realized that my other friends had been right. The schedule was very rigid. We had to wake up at 5:00 A.M. to the sound of the horn, rush to get ready along with a huge crowd, make a dash for our morning training, followed by a strict arrangement of lining up for breakfast, then we had to put in hours of training in the hot summer sun as well as attend some lectures. At night we slept in the classrooms of the school where camp was being held. I was unable to complete the twenty-one days at camp. After one week, I wrote a letter to my father:

Dear Dad,

It has been a week now that I am in Port Said. I have not had one night of uninterrupted sleep. Using the bathroom is next to impossible, because of the huge number of students and the very tight schedule they put us on. The recreation plans are nonexistent, and the level of hygiene is less than desirable.

Please forward my love to all.

Sincerely,
Mary

I had no idea what this letter would sound like to a father concerned about his daughter's health and well-being. I thought that I was simply furnishing him with news. The morning after he received the letter, I was called out of a lecture hall and informed over the loudspeaker that my father was at the camp director's office. I left the lecture hall amid many envious eyes and expressions.

When I arrived at the main office, my father asked me, "Do you want to come home with me, Mary?" I said, "Yes!" I brought my suitcase and headed out of what had seemed like a prison for the past nine days.

I learned from my father that when he'd received my letter he hadn't wasted a minute. He bought a train ticket right away and headed to the camp area. When he arrived at the gate, he was stopped because the camp organizers handled the grounds as if they were a war zone. Parents were not supposed to take their children, and children were not allowed to leave the camp. But my dad handed the guard his business card and asked him to take it to the person in charge, which he did. The military woman did not hesitate. In fact, she was rather anxious and concerned, because my father, though employed as a civilian, held a senior post at Egypt's military Border Guard Headquarters in Cairo. Guarding all Egypt's borders was a job held in special respect by people such as those running this training camp.

Once I was freed, it took me nine days, in and out of sleep, to recover. Just like a prisoner of war, I had to receive some intensive health care, and I never stopped thinking, if this was only a summer camp for teenage girls, how much worse would being in the army in a real war be?

When the school year started again I was one of the four girls who carried a gun, marched to the flagpole, put up the flag, and shouted "Long live the United Arab Republic" while the rest of the students repeated the same salute three times. (Since 1958 Egypt had been half of this union, along with Syria. The United Arab Republic dissolved, though, the following year, in 1961.) After the school's verbal salute to the flag, we four would perform the traditional military salute, responding to orders given by our military training teacher: gun to shoulder, to the side, to the front, back to shoulder position again, then turn around and march back to "headquarters" to store the guns securely and go to our classrooms to start our school day.

I continued with my high-school education, and I enjoyed challenging myself to obtain the highest grades possible. I knew that if I didn't study, I would do poorly. As stated earlier in this book, I was never praised for good grades like other students were, because the teachers were familiar with my older sisters and brother. And when I didn't study and got poor grades I was never reprimanded as the other students were. That was either because the teachers thought it was just a one-time mishap or because I was often absent, sick with my allergies.

For the last year in high school I decided to concentrate on four out of my eight classes, the four required for graduation, and to get my good grades in those. I planned to do that by switching schools to one that offered the chance to take only a few selected courses instead of doing the all-day program; many students were doing this at the time. The English School (another one of the originally British institutions) offered a choice of evening courses. So during the summer of 1963 my father approved my attending the following school year as an evening student.

By the end of the summer my dad fell sick with a heart condition that had haunted him mildly for the previous year or so. This time it was so severe, he was in bed. Physicians were in and out of our home constantly. I went for my interview at the English School one evening, when he was already unconscious. When I returned home I did not really want to turn the key in the door and let myself in, for fear of what might be waiting for me inside. Cousins and friends were all over the place. When I got in, I found that his condition was the same as when I had left.

That was October 1963. Samia and Nabil had been married for one year and were expecting their first child. During the late summer, Mother had become very ill. Apparently, a reaction from the stress of caring for my father. This left me in charge of calling doctors, buying the medicines, following schedules, and informing our caring guests of all the changes and conditions—all this while waiting for my seventeenth birthday, which was approaching. That birthday marks the age of adulthood in Egypt as eighteen does here in the United States.

I could not escape my situation. Once in a while, I would walk out on the balcony and close the door behind me. That way, people in the house wouldn't know where I was, and I could avoid hearing the dialogue going on inside the apartment. I would look as far down the road as I could see and wish I were there, leaving behind me all the pain and sadness. I was sad and scared, and I felt that normal life was only something to wish for and dream about. Finally, Mother got better and out of bed.

On the morning of October 4, 1963, a cousin came over to see my father. As I looked at my unconscious father, I said to the guest what I thought was true, "He looks better today, doesn't he?" My cousin nodded, and in a dejected manner responded, "Yes," then left the room. Soon after this brief conversation, I was standing next to my dad's bed, wanting to talk to him but knowing there would be no response, when two of his sisters walked in. Suddenly they screamed at the same time.

THE VISITOR

For five minutes, I gazed at my sick, sleeping father.
On the fourth day of the month,
The third day of his sickness,
Two aunts walked in.
One minute later they let out a scream,
Unraveling every nerve, muscle, and joint.
My heart raced, my body stood still.
My mind silently said, "He is resting."
Their loud screams said, "He is dead."

Was I gazing at my dead father?
Had death walked in silently before I did?
I thought I was alone with you,
But you had an unwelcome guest.

> One that drops in uninvited,
> Forces an ugly hand, freely picks and chooses,
> Forever changing the lives of the living,
> Taking away the least suspecting.
> DEATH, I WISH YOU WERE DEAD.

I felt lost, and asked my mother, "What do we do now?" Up until then, she had been holding up well. She left me, saying, "You are making me cry," and she turned her attention to the demands and the formalities of the situation. All I wanted to do was close my eyes and make it all into a bad dream.

Many of our friends came over and were helpful in every way. For the three months after the death, all our income was frozen by the government, a legality to enable the authorities to legalize all papers, income, and to designate my mother as head of the family since I was still underage. Once this process was complete, my mother would be awarded a pension from my father's job, which would include a stipend for my support until I reached adulthood. Our friends continued to give us advice and keep us company. However, I felt that all my father's friends had jumped in, trying to replace my father. After having just one father, I had more like five or six, and I did not like that at all.

I went to the police department and applied for an adult ID nine days after my father's death, the day of my seventeenth birthday. I had to process papers, forms, and get signatures of adults, list their positions at work, and so forth. This process in Egypt takes a long time because of the red tape, but I was very persistent. I took the forms to the father of one of my friends and got my ID sooner than anyone expected. I was then able to take care of all transactions, financial and otherwise, without the assistance, signatures, or approval of any of my late father's friends.

In Egypt, the family of the deceased has to be ready to receive guests in mourning for a full forty days after the death. On that fortieth day, a special Mass is held at church, preceded by a gathering of the whole family, friends, and neighbors for a feastlike meal at the home, served by the family in mourning. The timing has a religious background, based on how Jesus ascended into heaven on the fortieth day after his resurrection. It symbolizes that our dead, too, will rise. Thus the celebration.

On the eve of that fortieth day, one paternal aunt and my maternal aunt came over to spend the night with us so that in the morning they would be present to give us a helping hand upon the arrival of our guests. I was awakened after I went to bed by one of my aunts, and told that Nabil, my brother-in-law, had come over to ask my mother and her sister to join him as Samia was about to have her baby. They wanted Mother to be there to greet her first grandchild. I was given the instructions for the next morning: what to do in case Mother and her sister were not back before the rented chairs were delivered and the first guests came to stir, once again, our already wounded emotions. Off went Mother and her sister, and I went back to sleep, knowing that once again a load had been placed on my shoulders.

In the morning the chairs arrived, and the guests started to trickle in. There was no sign of Mother and my aunt for a frightening length of time. When they finally did show up, I was informed that the baby had not been born yet. (Babies do not follow family schedules.) Just before it was time to go to church for the special Mass, a telegram came. I was used to receiving sympathy telegrams by this time, so I ran downstairs to sign for it. I read it and found that it was good news for a change. It was from my brother in England, informing my father and the family that he had successfully achieved my dad's dream. He had been awarded the highest certification in medicine, a Fellow of the Royal College of Surgeons. We had not told my brother and sister that my father had passed away because we knew that he was getting ready for this very important examination.

To keep this a secret had been my job. I had to sit down by my uncle and write letters that sounded as normal as possible without mentioning my father's death. My uncle would dictate the ideas to me in Arabic, and I would translate them and write them in English, like the following:

Dear Samir,

Today Uncle Aziz and family came to visit us. We had a lovely lunch prepared by Mother. I was asked to write to you because the letter will be in English and you can read it quickly, rather than struggling with reading Arabic and taking more time than you can afford. We know how busy you must be. So this is just to let you know that all is well and when you are done with your exams, we will write you longer letters with more news.

> *Love,*
> *Mary and all the family*

This was clearly written under a lot of pressure. It made me feel like a prisoner of war, forced to do what I was told to do, not what I wanted to do.

The arrival of that particular telegram and the anticipation of the arrival of the first grandchild on the very day when tradition insists on the renewal of sorrow hit me like lightning. I managed to bring myself upstairs to the apartment and sat on the first chair near the door, but apparently I fainted, because when I regained consciousness, I was seated in a different room. Some guests made comments, saying that I should know how to handle the situation better. I wondered to myself, *How would they deal with the situation if they were in my place? How much emotion can a human being tolerate? This day would have been the best day of my father's life. He lived and waited for two happy occasions: his son's certification and the birth of his first grandchild. Instead of his being proud and happy, we are celebrating his spirit.*

We can go to extremes with our emotions and still be able to control them, but when opposite extremes pull against each other, we are bound to collapse emotionally, even if only temporarily.

After church, and after all the formalities of the fortieth day were completed, Mother and I went to visit Samia in the hospital, where we saw baby Emmanuel (Moni), a delightful little boy. As Moni was growing into a little boy, Samia wrote him a poem:

> My sweet little boy is Emmanuel,
> He's a joy to enjoy,
> A darling little boy.
> He listens and coos
> And hails the good news.
> When Dad's voice is heard
> He twits like a bird.
> He even thinks and ponders
> Like a person who wonders.
> Pray, Lord! Of what does he think?
> With his tiny fingers in link,

> Can anyone tell
> What's on the mind
> Of my sweet little Emmanuel?

The following summer my mother was advised to go to England to visit Isis and Samir, who were getting very restless and, needless to say, sad over the loss of our father and their delayed knowledge of that fact. Mother started to arrange for her trip and wanted me to join her. I wanted to go along too, but the government's policy was not to issue exit visas for young people. It was a waste of foreign currency, much needed during those years when Egypt was going in and out of wars.

Without being granted an exit visa from the Egyptian authorities, one could not apply for an entry visa to the foreign country to visit. That was the law and the law knew no exceptions. Mother wanted to cancel her trip but I insisted she carry on with her plans. Besides, that summer I was going to apply to enter a university, so I would be busy anyway. After she left, I had the option to stay with any of my uncles, aunts, or my sister Samia. I was not going to stay alone in our apartment.

Everyone was good to me. I visited them all, and I carried the keys to almost all their apartments, a gesture of welcome even when they weren't home. I must say that I was happy with all this, but deep inside happiness was not my true feeling. I was never sure why I felt the way I did at the time. Was it because of the loss of my father? That had been almost a year earlier. Perhaps it was because of my mother leaving me, although I had insisted she go?

I wondered if this was the way orphans felt: a sense of loss, of not belonging, topped with fear, sadness, loneliness, and anger all mixed together. At times, I felt that all those who loved me were not being honest, and that I had to take it upon myself to conquer those who seemed to be on my side as well as those against me.

That summer I was very busy gathering my application papers, and cutting through the red tape. I made up my mind that I would study English literature, not economics and bookkeeping, so, with Mother gone, that is how I filled out the forms. I think this was my first affirmative move toward my future.

After a month or so, Mother returned from England. She came back with gifts for me, clothes, and lots of very interesting stories about life in England.

The Beatles were at the height of their glory and I was a teenager, very eager to hear her stories, especially the one about the airport on the day she was leaving. The Beatles were at Heathrow as well, heading to the Continent on their first tour. She saw and described to me how the young women were screaming, some were even fainting, just as the papers depicted.

Mother thought it was total insanity, but I didn't want her to stop telling me about it.

Mother was feeling caught between cultural and social expectations. With my father dead and me still so young, many would expect her to marry me off as soon as possible. But since my father had put not only my brother through higher education but my older sisters as well, many others would criticize her for not following what would obviously have been his plan for me if she didn't help me go to university.

Seeing that my mother was divided between tradition and my continuing education, I told her my plan. I said I'd like to complete my higher education before getting married. That settled the matter.

And when the letter of acceptance from the Ain Shams University arrived, informing me of my enrollment in the School of Arts, my joy was overwhelming. Mother was understandably confused, since the School of Economics had been the plan when she'd left for England. I explained that I had decided while she was away that economics and bookkeeping were not for me. She accepted the choice I had made. But then another subject demanded our attention.

Friends and loved ones complained that when they came to visit us in that apartment, memories of my father's presence saddened them. Well, I thought, how much more was the place filled with memories for us who lived there? Mother was staying awake at night trying to reach a decision: should we move or stay? The people who cared about us, each and every one, wanted us to move. Each family said we should move next to them. We knew this was how they were expressing their kind feelings of goodwill. Realistically, though, if we did move, what area would be best?

One night when Mother was awake thinking, I gathered all my strength and I said to her, "If you get sick, I will be at a loss. No one other than the two of us can tell what we should do or where we should live. Moving next to anyone will provide company, but that is not all we need. We have to look for where our places of interest are. My college and the distance I will have to travel, as well as the accessibility of the places you use for banking and for social visits. That is what should determine where we move to." We decided to move into an apartment not too far from where we lived, in Heliopolis, a suburb also northeast of Cairo, about ten miles northeast of where we were in Qubba Palace.

My friend from high school, who was attending the same college, lived in Heliopolis too. Her name was Moushira, and she was very happy about my moving close to her. She lived with her mother and her two younger brothers; her father had died many years earlier. Her mother was employed by the Shell Oil Company in Cairo, a very successful executive secretary. The whole family was happy that Moushira would have a friend after school to keep her company, study with her, and go out for recreation with her while her mother was at work and her live-in housekeeper attended to the younger brothers and the home.

When the school year was over, and early that summer, we moved from the apartment where I was born and grew up, and where my father had died less than two years earlier. Once the moving was complete, we settled into our new apartment and the new school year was about to start. Even though it was my second year in college, I was not studying second-year courses. The first year had been an exceptionally difficult one for me. The loss of my father, the pressure caused by where we should live next, and with the usual problems first-year students experience all took their toll on me. I passed all my English language and literature courses, but we also had to take a course in social sciences, which was taught in Arabic. We were not a very strong group of students in the Arabic language; we were all graduates of English schools. Our instructor was annoyed by us and vowed to give us poor grades, which he did. I was given a grade that was one point short of passing.

We also had to take Arabic literature. Our professor was very kind to us; instead of teaching us Arabic literature in the Arabic language, he used English terms to explain and teach it. He wanted to help us understand, and none of us realized that doing this didn't help us. Instead, we were left with no literary vocabulary to use on our exam papers. As for French, Moushira and I studied together. We were given four stories throughout the year. We had to read, study, and examine each: the literary aspects, the vocabulary, and the grammar. We knew from students who had taken that course before that the exam was based on two of the stories and that students got to choose one of them to work with.

Planning on this, Moushira suggested that we leave out the most difficult one and concentrate on the other three. That way, we would be sure one of the three would be included in the final exam. Her plan appealed to me and we studied accordingly. When the day of the French exam arrived, we went in very sure of ourselves, only to find out that the whole sheet of questions were about the one story we had left out completely.

Moushira drowned in a flood of tears but I froze, sitting still in my seat. The inspector, out of pity seeing all her tears, whispered to me to help her out. I told him, "We studied together." We failed French and social studies, and because Moushira was tutored in Arabic literature throughout the year, she passed the Arabic course. I did not.

The university system at the time dictated that a student who failed one or two courses could continue on with the courses taught at the next year's level while taking the failed first-year courses over. But if a student failed more than two courses, he or she had to spend the whole school year working on just those courses.

It was a long year. Some friends suggested I get a job. Mother was not very pleased about this idea as she feared I would get involved in work and enjoy making money and not continue my education. Work and study together was not the common practice in Egypt. She was also concerned that if I was working, the government would discontinue the income I received from my father's pension and then I would be unable to leave work to go back to school.

Over Mother's mild objections, I applied to work for Pfizer Pharmaceutical Company, Cairo branch, and went for an interview. The manager was sitting at his huge mahogany desk. The air-conditioning unit was running and keeping the office comfortably cool, a rather rare situation in Cairo at the time, because only movie theaters were air-conditioned. He asked me if I knew how to type both English and Arabic. I explained that I had only been taught how to type English and that the job advertised had asked for English typing, not both languages, so that was why I had applied. I thanked him for his time and, silently, for the few minutes of air-conditioned comfort. Then I left.

Another friend told me of a job at the Vietnamese embassy. She thought that they wanted someone to translate from and into the English and the Arabic languages. When I went for my interview, I found that they wanted someone with a strong background in French, not English. This relieved my mother from yet another concern. I was totally unaware of the political situation, but she knew there was a war going on at the time between North and South Vietnam, and that the United States was involved on one side and the then Soviet Union on the other —a very serious matter when it came to an Egyptian citizen working for one or the other of those embassies. Egypt at the time had a strained political relationship with the United States and was pro–Soviet Union. All employees of foreign governments were followed daily by unidentified government people to monitor their activities at all times even while not at work, and my mother did not want any of that type of interference in our lives. Since I was not qualified for this second job, I did not apply. This was all the job searching I ever did in Egypt.

I devoted my academic year, then, to improving my Arabic and French. I took some private lessons in both languages, and I read a large amount of English literature on my own so that the year would not be, in the area of my academic interest, a total loss.

8
College, Trips, and Riots

I enjoyed my college years very much and would not have missed them for anything in the world. I was able to get in some excursions, travel, and celebrations, but those years were mixed with some unpleasant political disturbances, riots, and a war.

The Department of English Literature and Language, headed by our chairman, Dr. Louis Marcos, enjoyed a lot of social activities. The one that stands out in my memory was our excursion to Luxor and Aswān.

We left Cairo during the winter break by train, heading to upper Egypt. (The south and north in Egypt are referred to as upper and lower because of the nature of the land: the south has higher land whereas the north, or the delta, has low land.) After a long train ride we arrived in Luxor. We did not waste any time, as we wanted to see all that our ancestors had left behind, and to see the subject of one of my sister Samia's poems:

LUXOR

Luxor now is the Thebes of old,
With ancient walls and crowns of gold.
The Valley of the Kings has wonders in a row

> And the queens also have a valley to show:
> On the western bank many temples rank,
> From reign to reign, all secrets sustain.
> Of worship, of love, of war, and of peace,
> Each with a charm their laud increase.

We visited the magnificent tomb of King Ramses, where we had to walk miles underground. All the walls were painted, and the colors were still clear and shining. They showed the gods and goddesses; a bird representing the spirit of the king; and crops, date palms, olive trees, and wheat, detailing all that the king had in readiness for his next life.

We saw how the ancient Egyptian women wore their makeup and their jewelry. They wore heavy eye makeup: dark blue eye shadow, thick black eyeliner (kohl)—the same way they are portrayed in movies in recent history. This has left its effect on today's Egyptian women. Although they do not wear it as heavily as their predecessors did, eye makeup is very important to them.

Jewelry was also very important to ancient Egyptian women. They wore a lot of decorative jewelry all over their bodies—on their heads; on their wrists, sometimes all the way up to their elbows; then on the upper arm as well; and often around their ankles too. This style also is still important in the lives of Egyptian women today, especially for the *falaheen,* or the country folks. They love their gold bracelets, earrings, and *kirdan,* that is to say, the wide gold necklaces.

In each painting, we also had the chance to examine the variety of wigs each queen owned, and how devoted they were to preparing for their second life.

The ancient Egyptians thought that death was temporary and that the spirit would return to live in the body once again. That is why they took out the organs, such as the heart and others, and preserved them in urns, which they placed on shelves alongside their jewelry and food, in the same room where their mummified bodies lay.

Egyptians today are still very conscious of their second life. They are reminded of it during their religious services. But they believe now that preparations should be made in the religious and spiritual areas of development, not in the physical. Food and jewelry are now usually reserved for the living. We were also impressed by our ancestors' advanced knowledge in medicine. They discovered the circulatory system, and the organisms that cause diseases. They were aware of the cycles of life, of body functions, the intricate process of pregnancy, treatment of various ailments, and of course, the preservation of the body.

In the area of astronomy, they established the solar calendar based on a year of 365 days and consisting of 12 thirty-day months, plus an additional 5 days to follow the 12 months. All this knowledge was painted on the walls of the tombs.

Their knowledge of architecture is something that still is a mystery today. Our eyes could not absorb the majestic temples, and our brains were unable to digest the clever ways of building underground when they had no electricity. We learned that they used mirrors to reflect the light of the sun to the depths they needed.

When we arrived at King Tutankhamen's tomb, it was only a few steps down, and there lay the golden casket. The paintings were as fresh and shiny as if the painters had just completed their job. The tomb was preserved partly by the excavation of King Ramses' tomb, which is next to it. The young king's tomb had been covered with all the earth that was dug up when the Great King's tomb was discovered, thus preserving the small tomb and saving it until a more recent time.

All the buildings were amazing and beautiful, but there was one simple building that spoke for itself. It was a mosque newly built on top of an ancient Egyptian temple, which had apparently been covered by sand and earth for thousands of years. The continuity was striking: that their purpose for building there was religious, one form of worship built on top of another. Sometime after the new Mosque was built, a desert sandstorm unveiled the building underneath. The lower building was yellowish in color and the new one an off-white.

We rode the *flukas* (small sailboats) on the Nile and were entertained by local country musical groups playing the *naay* (a wooden bamboolike flute). The tune of the *naay* blends in with the calm mood of the river, creating a serene, relaxing atmosphere. *Certainly,* I thought, *this is what inspired Samia to write her poem:*

EGYPT THE BLEST

Tiny sparrow, tell your tale
Of your flight through hill and dale.
How your tender wings prevail
O'er the fierce tempestuous gale.
Come, tiny sparrow, and build your nest
In the palms by the Nile, and take a rest.
Then chirp to the warmth and chirp with zest,
To thank the Almighty for Egypt the Blest.

We then traveled to Aswān, and stayed at the Old Cataract Hotel (a cataract is a rapids), a massive beautiful edifice by the banks of the Nile. We did not want to go on any trips. We just wanted to sit on the terrace at the hotel and soak in the beauty of the scenery, and allow our senses to digest the dream we were living—one in which calm waters were adorned by Fiala Island, a little isle of green right in the middle of the waters, directly facing the hotel.

We did give in to going on some trips to see the High Dam and the temple that was saved from drowning by being moved and reconstructed when the dam was built. The temple is called the Fiala Temple. We did not make the longer trip to see Abu Simbel, the great temple of King Ramses II, where four of his mammoth statues, two on each side, adorn the entrance to the temple. That giant building was also doomed to drowning by the Aswān High Dam in the 1960s, but thanks to the forty million dollars raised by the concerned international community, Abu Simbel was elevated 213 feet and thus kept dry.

We cruised the artificial lake, Lake Nasser, created by the building of the High Dam. It was not a huge lake, yet it was large enough for us to enjoy an hour's cruise. Since it lacked vegetation around it yet, like the other lakes and the Nile that we were getting used to, we thought it the least beautiful lake around.

At the hotel, we ran into some of our famous actresses and actors—Shadia and Emad Hamdi, along with others—also, some Russian actors and actresses. They were filming a movie about the High Dam. We had a chance to talk with them and to have our pictures taken. They autographed our photographs and postcards. Our spirits were so high, in the company of famous people, we said to each other, "Who needs Hollywood?" We were on top of the world!

When it was time for us to return to Cairo, we unanimously refused. We were able to convince Dr. Louis Marcos that we could call our homes to tell our families that we were extending our stay a couple of days. We took votes and won a couple of extra days of perfect pleasure.

On our way back from Aswān to Cairo, we were named by our chairman the Committee for Social Affairs and Excursions. That made us very happy. We planned many more trips, such as one to Al Fayyūm, a city about seventy miles southwest of Cairo. Its landmark was the large lake called Birket Qārūn (Lake Karoon), which made the area the largest oasis in the Western Sahara Desert. We planned trips to the Red Sea, the Suez Canal, and Ismailia. The committee also invited speakers to the department of English: authors, journalists, and social workers. We had open discussions concerning current issues: social, educational, and political.

In the summer of 1966 I took my first international trip. I was granted an exit visa as well as an entry visa to England. Mother and I left Cairo for London, where we were met by my sister Isis, whom I had not seen for almost ten years, and my brother, Samir. Also, we met Anne, my sister-in-law, Samir's wife, whom I had not seen at all before, and their one-year-old twins, Nadia and Mark. Isis and Samir looked at me the way a tourist in Egypt would look at the pyramids—I had grown beyond their imaginations.

It was a great visit in England. Isis rented an apartment for us on the second floor of a house. On the first floor there were doctors' offices, physicians with whom she worked at the hospital. One day, because he knew who we were, a doctor who was fixing something in his desk and needed a wrench came upstairs to ask us for one. Mother invited him in so that he wouldn't have to wait by the door while we got it for him. He thanked her, saying that he was in a hurry. Then he said, "I will have a glass of orange drink." We gave him a glass of orange drink (which was water to which we'd add a little orange flavoring because the water itself didn't taste good) and the wrench, and he left.

The next day Isis told us that Dr. Sills had told her that, because of his experience in the British army in Egypt, he thought that when you go to an Egyptian's home you had to accept an offer of food or drink, or you would be offending the family. This is true to a degree, but in his case, when he was at the door borrowing something and going to his office, this custom would not have applied. People go too far when they are trying to abide by rules that are not their own. We had a good laugh at Dr. Sills, who was really trying to do his best to respect our customs!

While in England that summer I toured London. We went to theaters, looked at Buckingham Palace, where we watched the changing of the guard, to Piccadilly Circus, to Trafalgar Square, and stood by Big Ben until we heard it chime (live, not on the radio). For the first time in my life, I got on the Underground. All that I had heard or read about England, I finally experienced for real that summer. We then traveled to Mansfield, near Nottingham, to visit my brother and his family. The English countryside with all its shades of green, its little mountains and valleys, made a continuous picturesque scene along the M1 (motorway). It was all very beautiful.

Once in the Mansfield area, we had many chances to go to Nottingham and watch plays at the (then new) Nottingham Playhouse. We went shopping during the day, and visited Lord Byron's home, Newstead Abbey.

There we strolled the gardens and toured the mansion. We saw a monument on the east side of the grounds and we walked toward it. It was decorated with poetry, and when we read the poems we understood that they were written for Lord Byron's dog, who was buried there.

Inside the abbey, in the hallway, there was a large portrait of the handsome white-and-brown greyhound. A tour inside the home took us to the library, where the collection of books was very large. Above one of the bookcases were two portraits: one of the poet's mother, the other was of the poet himself. We made a comment about how handsome he looked, and the tour guide could not agree more. He went on to tell us that Byron had a limp and was very self-conscious because of it. After enjoying every bit of our tour, I remembered that while in college we had read Keats and Shelley, but not Byron.

After visiting the abbey several times, however, I felt that I knew more about this poet than the ones I have studied. There is something about going to someone's home and looking at what they looked at, where they sat, and seeing what was more important to them in their personal life, that brings you close to them. I expressed some of this feeling in a poem:

VISITING THE ABBEY

The monument you built
And adorned with poetry,
For Boatswain the dog,
A trophy he is worthy of:
The faithful friend
Of a man hungry for emotion.
Your portrait revealed the charm,
But not the limp
Which wounded your pride.
Your destiny divided
As was your physique.
Like an alchemist you transferred
Your bitterness and pessimism
Into literature and poetry,
Then spread it in Britain,
And also in Italy.

It was my first experience abroad and I enjoyed every minute of it. I wished that all my college life could be this good, but we have to live through some tough times as well as the good ones.

We were not spared the riots and the mention of war once back on campus. The unrest was caused by political tensions, and the country was in a state of alert ready for imminent war. Young recruits were kept in the military for indefinite lengths of time. The army and the reserves (those who were trained but not armed at the time) were on alert, so they couldn't go on vacation or leave the country.

Students questioned their future, as to whether they were going to end up in the army and stay there for an undetermined length of time, or whether they would have jobs and be able to lead normal lives. We all wanted to know the answers to our questions. That was the normal attitude of people that age at that time. Constant fear of imminent war was a very difficult way of living. We felt that this inability to predict our future was not fair.

The following school year, riots broke out once again. At that time Anne and the twins, who were two and a half years old by then, had just arrived to visit us in Cairo. When they came, I still had two more weeks in the semester, then I'd have a two-week break. Our guests were staying for a month, so I would have some time to show them around, but I really wished I could take them sightseeing right away and not have to go to school. It seemed like torture to have to attend my classes the morning after their arrival, and I was thinking as I left for school that I'd give anything to get time off. I didn't know yet that, in a way, my wish was going to be granted.

As we were in class that morning, attending a history of the English language course, we heard loud shouting. Some university students were demonstrating in the courtyard, and soon we heard the police fire shots into the air to separate the crowd. Dr. Ausalie carried on with the class; he did not want to let us leave. The noises intensified rather than dying down. Finally he sent a student out to investigate and return with news.

The student came back with tears running down his cheeks, blinking to find his way back into the classroom. He said that teargas had been used, and it made such a heavy cloud, he couldn't tell exactly what was going on, because he couldn't see. That convinced our professor to let us leave. If the police were using teargas, arrests would follow. We students who didn't want to join the riot hoped it was not too late to escape.

Ain Shams University is built on the site of one of King Farouk's palaces, in Abassya, a nearby northern suburb of Cairo. On its vast grounds were housed three schools—Law, Sciences, and the Arts—as well as a central library, school offices, and Administration. The rest of the university's schools, such as the medical school and its adjoining hospital and the school of engineering, were nearby, but off the palace grounds. Our three schools, however, were surrounded by a decorative iron fence, and the police had closed the gates, locking up the rioting students along with those like us who were not involved.

We were determined to escape because we did not want to spend the night in prison, nor did we want to be questioned by authorities for something we didn't even do. Needless to say, we were terrified.

Then it dawned on us that there was a gate on the back alley that we used as a shortcut when we were in a hurry to get to the closest metro station to go home. We rushed back there, saying, "If that gate is still open it will be the gate to our salvation." The gate was ajar, but the police were about to close it. Narrowly escaping stones thrown at the police and angry groups pushing and pulling, we slipped out, catching what we found later to be the last metro train coming from downtown and going to Heliopolis.

Similar riots by Cairo University students, who started from Giza, the southern suburb of Cairo, had spread to the public transportation, shutting it down. Cairo was at a standstill due to the students, who were uncontrollable. I got home and cheerfully told Mother and Anne that there would be no school for a few days—maybe even for the two weeks until midyear break, if the authorities decided to give the students a longer cooling-off period, as they had during last year's riots.

The university did close for a full month, during which time the authorities met with student leaders and groups to calm them down. As for me, my plans for recreational tours were already in process in my head!

Because we lived in a suburb, we were away from all the activity in the city. It seemed so calm and peaceful where we were. That same day, I took Anne and the twins and went out as I had wished. We used cabs for transportation and stayed in the suburb for the day, saving down town for another day.

When we returned, Mother signaled me to go to the kitchen. By the look on her face and the signal, I knew it was not good news. She told me that Moushira, my friend, had come over to our house while I was gone. She had needed some company, someone to talk to about her experience on campus earlier that day. She had detailed to Mother every little move.

The story had been shocking to Mother. She had not imagined that we'd been in danger of being locked up on campus, since I hadn't mentioned any details. Moushira's brother, though, had been locked up until the following morning because he was involved in the riot. Families couldn't do anything for their relatives except wait for the authorities to release them.

When I told Mother that all of what Moushira had said to her was indeed true, she became very upset, first at me because I hadn't mentioned any of it, and secondly at herself, because she hadn't believed Moushira when she was telling her the story. I felt bad about how I had handled the situation. Apologetically I told Mother that "all's well that ends well." I had only been trying to save her worry over both my danger that morning and our proposed outing that afternoon.

Since my break from school was extended, Anne, Nadia, Mark, and I took off to the Mediterranean seaside city of Alexandria to enjoy the peaceful beaches. It was not yet vacation time for the general public, so the resort was not crowded and our stay was most pleasant.

After the long vacation and our guests' safe return back to England, classes resumed and the school year was completed.

The following school year was relatively quiet in the sense that there were no riots, but tensions were felt everywhere. The political scene was not peaceful. War was imminent and was felt in every speech given by President Nasser.

This was 1967, and the few years of peace we'd had since the war in 1956 did not last any longer. Nasser once again got nervous about the military situation between Syria and Israel and hastened to pull the United Nations Emergency Force out of the east side of the Red Sea, a matter which aggravated the overall situation in the Middle East. It especially disturbed Israel. Egypt was attacked severely during the Six-Day War and suffered a setback, from which the area is still struggling to recover to this day. Israel took over the Sinai, the East Bank of the Jordan River, and the zone around the Gulf of Aqaba, lands traditionally held by Jordan or Egypt.

When I had completed my end-of-year exams, I got myself ready the following morning to go visit my cousins who lived across town. We heard a siren, and Mother asked me not to leave the house because, she said, I might get stranded on the way if shelling started. I told her I was sure it was only a horn on one of the new metro cars—drivers enjoyed making them sound like sirens—and it was just a game of war.

As we were discussing whether I should stay, the bombing started, so there was no question. It was war. And we were living even closer than before to the recruiting center, the military and civic airports, and the military academy.

We turned on the radio. All the stations were playing military music. I knew from the last war that when military music was played in place of regularly scheduled programs, it meant one of two things: either the death of an important person, such as the President, or WAR. I was now convinced that this was the real thing, not a game.

"Let's pack our suitcases and go to Uncle Aziz's home," I said to Mother. I was remembering my father's decision to go there during the 1956 war, and how it had comforted us all. This time we were two women alone; we had to take action by ourselves. It was a frightening moment, but we did get ready.

We had packed and walked downstairs to ask the porter to call a cab when the ground started to shake beneath us. The sound of the bombing was deafening. When the peak of the attack calmed down, we were able to call a cab. We headed toward my uncle's home, taking the back streets, away from the heavy shelling.

On our way, we saw trucks, buses, military equipment, and many, many young men heading toward their appointed destinations, from where they might or might not return. I felt very sad for them.

When the cab turned the corner onto my uncle's street, we looked at their balcony and there they were, the whole family stretching their necks out, looking in anticipation of our arrival. Though we had not phoned, they had known we'd show up sometime soon.

Throughout this new war we sat there, listening to the news. Mother would hear about the number of planes that were downed by either side and she would cry. When it was the "enemy," I would tell her, "Mother, that's not our side." She would answer, "So what? Aren't they human, too? Don't they have families and loved ones just as we do? And what about their youth? Isn't it a waste that they are dying and won't live a full life?" Then I would say to her, "I do agree with your point, but let us be practical. We will cry for our people and let them cry for theirs. If we don't do it this way we will run out of tears."

After the losses of the Six-Day War, Nasser tried to resign. But the people of Egypt would not allow him to do it. There are several reasons and theories with regard to the situation. One was that people thought no one would be able to fill the position in such a powerful manner as he did. Another was that he had brought the country into this disastrous situation, why should he have it so easy and sit back while the people tried to pull themselves together once again? They felt that he should be the one to suffer the consequences of his deed.

Whether it was one reason or another, the result was that Nasser withdrew his resignation and remained president of Egypt until his death in 1970.

The following school year was quiet, and in the summer of 1968 I left Egypt for England as soon as my exams were over. This time Mother was in Egypt and I was the one traveling alone for the first time. That summer Samia, still living in Dokki (a suburb south of Cairo), was expecting her second child. After suggesting a choice of names, I took off and waited for the information to come in the mail about the arrival of the baby. At the end of July, the happy news of the birth of Mary Therese came from Samia as follows:

> OUR DEAR LITTLE MEME
>
> Sleep, my pet, sleep soundly too.
> Sleep, my pet, for I love you.
> As your breath comes quick and warm
> I try to smother down the storm
> For though your tiny form so dear
> Is cuddled in my arms so near,
> Still I feel you're miles away.
> Do quickly wake and with me stay.
> O Sleep! Indeed you are so strange.
> Do let us know what is your range.
> I see my pet sometimes with frowns,
> And sometimes tears run down her gowns.
> Whilst, oftimes, I see her smiles
> And these my worry soon beguiles.

I stayed with Isis and shared the room with her at the doctors' residence at Shrodells Hospital in Watford. I had a folding bed, which I pulled out every night to sleep on, and in the morning I hid it under her bed. I enjoyed this experience very much, but after a month of going back and forth from Watford to Mansfield, where my brother and his family lived, and touring London, Stratford-upon-Avon, the Isle of Wight, Bournemouth, riding the hovercraft, visiting Lord Byron's Newstead Abbey again, plus the various zoo gardens and castles, I decided that it was time to go home to spend the rest of my summer vacation with my friends—unless I could get a job in England!

Isis tried very hard to help me, and she was successful in finding me a job where one of her junior residents' wife was working. This was at the John Dickinson paper company in Croxley Green, near Watford. I went for my interview with Mr. Thompson, a very respectable Englishman. When he smiled, it was a condescending gesture not really sharing the joy. He questioned me about my future, telling me that since I had a sister and a brother who were doctors, what did I plan to be? I told him that was why I was looking for a job, in order to decide my future. He let me understand that I would get the job, which I did. I received a call later from his office informing me of when to start work.

9
Work in England, Returning to Egypt, and the Wedding

I felt the presence of Charles Dickens from the very first day I started to work until the time I left. It seemed that the factories hadn't changed since his days, which provided me with a sense of familiarity that came from reading his novels. The only major difference, which *was* very important, was the absence of children working at the factory. This, I thought, was partly the result of his efforts and critical writings. The absence of the youngsters proved to me the power of the author and of the written word.

In my own mind, I assigned names to some of the people working at John Dickinson, names Dickens had given his characters, such as Uriah Heep with his red hair, eyelashes, and eyebrows. The seemingly unhealthy atmosphere of the place made me feel as if we were living in nineteenth-century England. I liked being there very much, though I knew it was only temporary.

On payday I would pay for my whole week's lunch, as that was the system. Then I would leave work and go to the stores, and spend all the rest of my money on clothes. I did not have to save my bus fare for the following week; Isis gave it to me daily. Soon I had too many clothes to be able to take home with me on the plane.

It so happened that my brother-in-law, Nabil, stopped for a brief visit. He was in England on a business trip, as was often the case. I asked him if he would take a suitcase full of clothes back home for me. He agreed, and that solved my problem. I did not realize, however, the effect this would have on my mother until I received a letter from her, the tone of which reminded me of Mr. Doolittle's reaction to the news that his daughter Eliza's clothes had been burned.

My mother's concern was that since I had a job and I was making money, buying new clothes, and did not even need the ones I brought from home, that I would never consider returning home to complete my last year of college to qualify for the B.A. degree. I assured Mother that I would return to Egypt once the school year started.

While Nabil was in England, he visited my brother in Mansfield. He complained of a cyst in the upper lid of one of his eyes, so Samir took him to his office and removed it for him. Not major surgery by any means, but just a little discomfort. After his surgery, he got on the train from Nottingham to Watford and stopped to see us for a few hours. It was strange, but that morning, I had had minor surgery, too. The doctor removed a little bone from my toe joint. A bone that had built up after an exercise incident with Samia years before: We had been exercising, and our feet bumped into each other. We were both in great pain. Soon my toe was swollen and it turned blue. I could not even tolerate a breeze of gentle air on it. I refused medical treatment on the grounds that I had only hit it against my sister's foot, not a piece of furniture or other hard object. After more than a year of waiting for it to heal, I was left with an extra piece of bone, which gave me a lot of pain and caused me to limp after a short walk.

On the day when my surgery was planned, I was supposed to take general anesthesia, and I was ready. However, after a long wait, I had to have my surgery under local anesthesia because the anesthesiologist was called to attend to an emergency. I got so scared that I could not control my knees from knocking against each other, which amused the resident surgeon quite a bit.

When Isis came to pick me up, expecting me to be asleep or maybe just starting to wake up from sedation, I was wide awake. Her eyes opened wide. She asked me, "How soon did you get up?" And I told her what had happened. She informed me firmly that she would take me to her room in the residence to rest. She was on her way to the dentist because of a tooth that had been giving her a rough time. She had been on antibiotic treatment and this was the day she was scheduled to have it extracted. I told her that I needed no rest. I was going with her to the dentist to keep her company. After all, extracting a tooth is no fun.

At the residence, one of the doctors' wives offered to go along with Isis so I could rest. She said she would drive Isis back if need be. She also assured me that she would take good care of her, and I should rest after my surgery. I could not accept staying behind, so I went along with both of them. I sat in the back so that I could stretch out my leg on the backseat, to avoid pain and swelling.

We waited for Isis in the car while she dashed in and out of the dentist's office. As she was running toward the car, the lady commented, "Oh, she didn't have it extracted." Isis got behind the wheel and drove while we were asking her why she didn't have it removed, but she nodded to indicate she had. She was unable to elaborate as her mouth was closed, holding the gauze over the wound to control bleeding. The lady could not stop herself from telling us what a strange family we were!

When we arrived back at the residence, we received the call from Nabil telling us that he was at the train station in Watford, coming to visit with us.

We picked him up and returned to Isis's residence, where we made our own mixed ward. He needed to rest his head and close his eyes, but he could talk and felt well; I needed to stretch my leg, otherwise I felt fine; Isis sat by the sink with a cup of mouth rinse. Each one of us took the position most comfortable and we were all in good spirits, each swallowing pain reliever when needed. When it was time for Nabil to catch the train to go back to his hotel in London, all three of us got in the car. Resuming our positions, Isis stuffed her mouth with the absorbing cotton and silently drove, I sat in the backseat and stretched out my leg, and Nabil sat in front with his eyes closed till we dropped him off at the train station.

I was in England for a little over four months, and they were filled with interesting happenings. One evening at 7:00 P.M.—suppertime at the doctors' residence—the maid was walking up and down the halls, ringing a handbell, making sure every doctor heard it, whether in their rooms, in the library, or in the TV room, announcing that dinner was being served. As we were heading toward the door to go and eat, the phone rang. Isis had to attend to an emergency.

I continued on to the dining room because by then all the doctors knew who I was. I took a seat at the dinner table, which happened to be across from a Dr. White, when a fly came zooming in, heading toward the main dish, which was a large oven tray in the center of the table that held sliced potatoes. I shooed the fly. That prompted Dr. White to say to me, "It's all right, Miss Rizk, this fly is British, it doesn't carry any disease like the ones in Egypt." I heard him but I kept my silence. An Iranian ear, nose, and throat doctor responded, saying to Dr. White, "Egyptians are good people. They are descendants of a single race, that of the pharaohs." He then continued, saying, "Iranians are also from a single race."

Dr. White was not content to leave the conversation at this point. He persisted. "The British are a collection of the *best*; therefore, the British *are* the best!"

I made it a point after that not to join them at the dinner table if Dr. White was present.

During my long stay with Isis, I had many opportunities to observe her on duty. There was an exchange transfusion on a baby just a day or two old. Another was a deformed baby, just born and rushed in an ambulance to London to receive the advanced care that was necessary for its case. After these observations, I did not once regret my choice to study English literature. When I went with her to St. John's Hospital in Hemel Hempstead, I thought of the poet John Keats and wondered if he had ever visited this hospital when he lived in Hemel

Hempstead, with his friend Charles Brown in 1818, before sailing to Italy in 1820.

My brother, his family, and my sister wanted to go on a vacation. The decision was made that we would go and spend a week at a farmhouse. This was a rather large farm and the house was open for guests during the summer as a bed-and-breakfast. The farm, in Devon, which is in southern England, was named after its owners' name, Yendel. This was a new experience for me. My sister and I were given a room outside the main house. It was a converted pig barn, along with three or more other rooms attached to each other. The Yendels' summer business had grown in size, so they had had to expand. I had not wanted to leave my job to go on this vacation, as I had just started to work and had no vacation days. I did go with them for a long weekend, and I was able to ask for a brief sick leave due to the problems I was having with my toe. I stayed for that short time and was happy to catch the train and return to Watford. The impression this trip left on me was very strong, especially because Mark, my little nephew, unable to say *Devon*, called it *Heaven*, which made us laugh at the irony.

HOLIDAY IN HEAVEN

Brits call it Devon
Mark called it Heaven.
The Yendels' farm swells
With summer vacationers.
The sheep are busy fattening,
The cows just returned from milking.
The air in the drawing room,
Pregnant with smoke and dust,
With families and honeymooners.
The evening tea is brewing.
At long last, it is bedtime.
Ten P.M., one more day has ended!
All is dark and peaceful.
Then, the dreaded walk to the outhouse.
Dark, damp, animal odor
Treading the cows' footsteps.
The light switch on,
The generator shakes the house
Like an earthquake measuring six to eight.

> Mary Yendel yells from her upstairs window,
> Waking every guest up.
> "If the lights did all this
> What will the flush do?"
> Devon, they called you *Heaven*?!

I stayed with my job at John Dickinson for as long as I could, but I was facing more problems than I had expected. My visa was a visitor's visa and that did not permit me to work. I had taken my passport to the Home Office to change my visa from visitor to a different type that would allow me to work. My passport stayed at the Home Office until it was time I wanted to return to Egypt, so I called and asked for my passport back. They sent it to me without changing the visa status.

On my last day on the job, Mr. Thompson's secretary called me to answer a phone call. This was unusual because when Isis telephoned me she always contacted the department where I worked, and I didn't know anyone else who would call me at work. The call was from the Home Office and the conversation went as follows:

OFFICER: Is this Miss Rizk?
MARY: Yes.
OFFICER: Is this Miss Mary Rizk?
MARY: Yes.
OFFICER: Is this Miss Mary Nessim Rizk?
MARY: Yes.
OFFICER: Do you know that you are not supposed to be working?
MARY: Yes, but I resigned and this is my last day.
OFFICER: And when are you leaving the country?

When this question had been asked three different ways, as he had done with my name, I told him:

MARY: Sir, I am leaving on Saturday morning on British flight number [I gave him the flight number] out of Heathrow [I also gave him the time of departure] if you would like to come and see me off.
OFFICER: No, no. I just want to tell you not to come back to this country unless you have a work permit.

That call was after I had been cross-examined earlier in the week by Mr. Thompson about why I was resigning:

MR. THOMPSON: What made you decide to leave us, Miss Rizk?
MARY: I decided to go back home and complete my education.

I could tell from his smirk that he was not mad at me, but rather at himself because he had believed, when he interviewed me for the job, that I was going to be there to work not just for the summer, but to make a career of it. After several questions about my future plans, he accepted my resignation, and I left his office.

My large wardrobe was then packed in four suitcases and several pieces of carry-on luggage, and off I left for Egypt, for my B.A., and for mother's peace of mind.

Getting off the plane, however, was an embarrassing experience. I blocked the way walking down the stairs of the plane and an employee ran up the stairs to give me a hand and get the passage cleared. When I arrived at the bottom of the steps, Nabil was waiting for me. He had not recognized that this awkward passenger was the one he was there waiting for! I was wearing a wig, and he had never seen me with long hair. Also, I had on a black coat, a gift from a friend in England for her mother, so I was practically in disguise!

I went back to the university to catch up on my studies. I had missed almost four weeks, which meant that a lot of hard work was ahead of me. I needed help from my friends and the faculty. There was no doubt I was going to receive it. I had good friends and I was, in a way, an asset to the English department. Not too many students visit England and return with information, material, and the latest news from Shakespeare's birthplace and the latest on the theaters in Stratford-upon-Avon and London. My absence was handled as part of the term spent abroad.

This was my final year and I was determined to make it my best year, both with my grades and my social life.

Isis arranged to visit Egypt during my midyear break. She had missed the cousins, friends, and the whole place very much after her more than ten years away. By then I was an expert on planning tours. I had traveled around enough to take her on a tour by myself, but it so happened that Mr. Nassar, my Arabic tutor, who was by then a friend of the family, was on an assignment to investigate the status of Shell Oil Company employees in Luxor and Aswān. So he helped me with more elaborate tours than I had originally arranged. During this trip, I remember, he completed writing his third novel, *Al Zobab Wal Khalaa*, a social piece, dealing with class and with socio-economic conditions in Egypt. His book amused me a great deal.

One of the tours he arranged for us was to have a company-chauffeured car pick us up at the hotel and take us on a tour of the new factories producing candy. The driver was dismayed to find that his guests were two women. The areas we were to visit were places where only men were permitted to enter.

We assured him that we did not have to visit the restricted places, and that we would be happy to go only to the open areas so that he would not get into trouble. But he insisted on taking us to where Mr. Nassar had asked him to take us. (We were not aware at the time that this young man was a Shell employee, whose work in chauffeuring would be reported to headquarters in Cairo as part of his job. He wanted to make a good impression on Mr. Nassar so he would be recommended for promotion.)

We got in the car and he said that not only were we women, but that we appeared to be more Western than Egyptian. I suggested we duck under the seats until we passed the checkpoint. He laughed and said that would be even worse. Our visit went smoothly, no problems, and nobody stopped us.

We visited the factories and had a look at the High Dam from each angle. The dam was now more complete than when I had visited it with my college group a couple of years earlier. At that time it had looked like a standard dam with nothing special about it. Now I noticed the huge electronic stations surrounding it, on the banks of the Nile, along with some more electronic equipment that, not being an engineer, I had trouble understanding. But all in all, the look was one of more power and majesty.

We enjoyed our stay in Aswān as much as we enjoyed Luxor and all its temples and tombs, then we returned to Cairo. Soon after we returned, it was time for Isis to leave us again for England. Mother and I had been under the false impression, given to us by well-wishers, that when she came home to visit she would feel how much she missed everything and decide to stay. This made it difficult for us to accept her return to work, and it intensified our painful feeling at this new separation.

Once the midyear break was over and Isis had returned to England, I had to attend to my studies and the intensive work. It was also time to start thinking and planning for my future. While my intention was to go to England for my master's degree, I noticed too that some of my friends were thinking of getting married, others were looking for jobs. Moushira, my friend, told me that she was getting married to an engineer. Her aunt knew him and thought he was the right person for her. She had told her aunt and her mother that she didn't love him, and they had replied, "Marry him now, love him later. He has a lot of money and that will guarantee your happiness." This way of thinking was very upsetting to me. I was surprised that her well-educated mother, who had put her daughter through college, would still believe in the value of an arranged marriage.

I imagined that the Egyptian bride's pledge to her family, society, and to her future husband, if written, would read as follows:

> My brain, I send for cremation.
> My tongue is still, no negotiation.
> My eyes are blind, except for what you see.
> My ears are deaf, except for what you hear.
> My appetite is tailored to fit your every craving.
> My soul I unroll, red carpet for your sole to tread.

A number of other friends were getting married as well, while others were emigrating with their families to either Canada or the United States. These were the peak years of emigration from Egypt, the 1960s.

In spite of the fact that the immigration doors were open in the United States, the political scene, with regard to Egypt and America, was very tense. So much so, that a group of extreme educators came up with the idea of eliminating the courses taught on American literature in the schools and universities in Egypt. Many of us saw this as a very narrow-minded way of looking at education.

There was a huge uprise from people who were more literarily enlightened, who said that education knows no political boundaries. If we canceled those courses, we would place ourselves deeper in the dark, and would start a decline in our educational system altogether. Our chairman, Dr. Louis Marcos, wrote an article in Egypt's main newspaper, *El-Ahram*, saying that if we were to take American literature out of our curriculum, we might as well cancel journalism, which is the voice of the people.

I agreed with Dr. Marcos and all those who defended teaching the courses in American literature. But then there was that voice, coming from somewhere in the back of my mind, telling me, "But that's one less course you'd have to worry about." That was a voice I did not heed too closely; it was the one of a lazy student. But every now and then it cried out under pressure.

The American literature course was rescued, thanks to the uproar, and I was more than happy because it turned out later that the only knowledge of the United States I had before coming here, I gained from reading some of its literature. The course introduced us students to some of America's culture, lifestyle, and ways of thinking, and to what made the country so different from Europe and other civilizations of the world. It prepared me somewhat—but not enough—for all that America would soon have to offer me.

Isolation topped the list of qualities we studied. The vast land was separated from the rest of the world by two large bodies of water, and that was how Americans liked it. This led to the next quality, which was individualism. Due to isolation, people of this country had to put their faith in themselves, and they developed their individuality, sometimes at the price of weakening family identity and tradition. Democracy was another, the total independence from the order of rank that Europeans abided by. Provincialism was a byproduct of America's isolation; besides not paying much attention to formalities, the United States also tended to discard the accepted viewpoints Europeans had, sometimes to its cultural detriment. Perhaps because this country was not yet rich with history, it seemed, too, to have a sense of inferiority in relation to the Old World, the sophisticated culture of Europe. Another all-American characteristic was the frontier ethic, from which I believe, today's American society, especially the American family, still suffers. The "get-up-and-go"—after the gold or the land or whatever was wanted—can often be at the expense of others. In the past this worked better than it does in today's more tame society.

"Because of all these characteristics," explained our professor, "and especially because of rugged individualism, the American individual is rather eccentric!" This comment amused every student, and perhaps increased the curiosity of every one of us with regard to the American personality.

We then studied the Colonial, the Romantic, and the Realistic periods in the American literary world. We were introduced to the Puritan writer Nathaniel Hawthorne, and we read *The Scarlet Letter*. Before reading Hawthorne, we had pictured America as always being the modern society it is today, not the society that was once Puritan. Reading this piece of literature led us to think that the American community, after all, was similar to the rest of the world and experienced what some societies, even now, are still experiencing.

Then we did a brief reading of the history of the plantations in the South and of the industrial North. This was a helpful background to reading Mark Twain's *Huckleberry Finn*. The author painted a vivid picture, dramatic and emotionally moving, of American racism; a clear reflection of a social problem unique, we thought, to American culture. "Not only does America have gold," we said, "but also problems of different colors, the colors of the people." Reading Twain's novel shed light on a piece of history that was important for everyone to understand in order to appreciate what is going on in today's America.

We read some of the plays by Tennessee Williams, and we compared the social and domestic American issues that he portrayed, with those of D. H. Lawrence's novels about British society.

We were also studying the writings of Naguib Mahfouz, a respected Egyptian novelist, later a winner of the Nobel Prize for literature (1988). From an Egyptian viewpoint he also dealt with these twentieth-century issues. All three authors wrote about the difficulties of personal relationships and of sexual maladjustment, and they were critical of middle-class culture. They dealt with these issues in the twentieth-century style, which was psychoanalytic.

In his novel *El Sarab,* Mahfouz presents Rabab, the heroine, a frustrated wife, and Kamel, the hero, a victim of society and middle-class culture. The characters in Mahfouz's literature are calmer and not as fiery as those of Williams.

We concluded that even though each of the authors had his own style and originality, the social problems each one of them was treating were similar—thus bringing three very different cultures together in their facing a universal problem.

When we read Walt Whitman's *Leaves of Grass*, we felt that we were finally looking into the America we had imagined it to be. We liked Whitman's originality, the free form of his poetry, which did away with metrics and with structure, the shedding of tradition for his new realistic approach to a happier and simpler way of life. Whitman was refreshing to us because he was more what we had expected the new land to bring to the world and to the arts.

In the middle of March graduation was only two months away, and tensions were building all around. A friend introduced me to a family friend of hers who was a physician training in New York. He was in Egypt visiting at the time, and wanted to meet an Egyptian young woman. I found myself doing what some of my other friends were doing: looking for a mate. When Gamil and I met, we found that we were both very enthusiastic about travel, an interest that has not faded since then.

We got engaged by the end of March, before he had to return to his work in New York. Engagement in our Coptic Orthodox Church is a formal, religious, family-attended celebration. Both the man and the woman wear wedding bands on their right hands.

Soon after my graduation in August, Gamil returned to Egypt for our wedding. That was when the priest switched the bands from our right hands to our left, making the wedding formal. Because Gamil's father had died earlier in the year, we could not have a big wedding party. Tradition dictates that the family of a deceased is not to celebrate happy events by a party or anything other than the religious celebration, for a minimum of one year. So a few days after our small wedding we left Egypt, and stopped in England for six days before continuing on to New York City to start our life in Brooklyn.

By contrast, my maternal grandmother's wedding, which was documented in E. L. Butcher's book *Egypt As We Knew It* (London: Mills and Boon, 1911), was celebrated in full tradition and in a very joyful manner.

Mrs. Butcher, a British missionary who lived in Egypt and knew my grandmother Miriam as a teenage woman, described in one full chapter entitled "Miriam's Wedding" the formalities and traditions of the time. We are now grateful for the description because some of those customs do not exist anymore —like the part of the ceremony where a bullock is executed, after which the bride has to step over the running blood (the flesh of the sacrificed animal was given to the poor). This was an offering by the bride's family, symbolic of continuous blessings that she would enjoy all her married life.

Mrs. Butcher also tells us in her book about the more pleasant wedding customs. The lane where the bride lived was decorated with palms, flags, and lanterns. The loud sounds of celebration were supplied by a brass band and by the traditional screams of joy that are called *zaggareet*. They sound like calls for help to the unfamiliar ear. Only some Egyptian women know how to produce this loud sound. Those who do open their mouths as if to pronounce the letter *o* and with some superb muscle control of the tongue, they move their tongues at a very fast pace from side to side while letting out a loud scream. The tongue acts like a musical instrument's string, creating a tune to what would otherwise be just screaming.

The author goes on to describe the festivities saying, "We all poured out of the church. I knew the wedding feast would last till midnight, and even then the bride's fatigues are not over. At an early hour next morning, she has to sit in state to receive the congratulations of her relations and friends, who each give her a piece of money." This tradition is still surviving.

Poems

JUGGLER

Sometimes I feel I am a juggler,
One that juggles cultures.
When Americans say "I don't know."
And Egyptians say "I know it all."
Loud and clear, Americans say, "I'm broke."
Broke Egyptians say, "I'm blessed with dough."
American parents tell their children,
"You're grown, you're on your own."
Egyptian parents tell their children,
"I'm your backbone."
Americans hug, Egyptians kiss,
What if I miss?!
I'd rather juggle fireballs,
Crystal vases, or china dolls.

A.M.   P.M.

"Smell the dust, Abla* Mary,
It's going to be a warm day,"
Said my driver
On the way to Cairo's airport,
"Sixty-six warm degrees"
On a winter day in January.
I inhaled the dust along with love
And boarded my flight for Chicago.
Sixteen hours later
I looked from my window.
We were landing,
A fresh coat of white fluffy snow
Had covered O'Hare field.
Dozens of little trucks
Racing as if in a maze
To clean the runways.
The icy cold air slapped my face
Upon stepping outside.
No dust. The freeze purified the air.
From continent to continent,
From extreme to extreme,
From home to home,
I extend and belong.

A title of respect for a woman

SAHARA

We flew over the mountains,
Green land and waters,
And when we saw gold dust,
We knew it was our homeland.

The pilot called,
"Get ready to land."
We now are over the Sahara sand.

On both sides of the Nile
The yellow arms are stretched
To welcome every guest,
To embrace the racing hearts,
With the warmth acquired
From the golden beams
That bounced all day,
And now radiate,
Interacting with our arrival.

Then all settles down in the west.
Soon, the sand loses its heat,
And a cool silver breeze
Responds to the silver moon.
A glow that soothes all blisters.

That is how the desert does it:
Gold in the morning,
Silver in the evening.

CHRISTMAS THEN AND NOW

We stuck cotton balls
On the windows from inside
And made believe it was snow.
The sun shone outside
And penetrated the windows,
But did not melt our snow.
We enjoyed the decorations
And mother nature's warmth.
We dreamt about what
A white Christmas would be.
In Wisconsin today
The snow is outside,
On the windows, the trees,
The houses, and all around,
The plow was even stuck
On our driveway one day.
We decorate our windows
With colored lightbulbs,
They glow from inside and shed light
On the snow that is outside.
And we sit indoors
In the warmth that blows from the vent
And admire the sight
Of the glow on the snow that will not melt.
Then we dream of the snow
That came from cotton balls
And the sun that shone,
And the warmth that penetrated the windows.

THE LOOFA TORTURE

It only took two years
And the loofa followed me.
The loofa always made a red tomato out of me.
My mother used to say, "Scrub your knees."
"Europeans don't use a loofa," I said,
So I bought a dozen sponges
And I said to mother, "See?"
My mother said, "Scrub your knees."
Then I came to the land of gold
And thought, "The loofa won't find me."
It only took two years
And the loofa followed me,
"I will not let the loofa ever torture me."
But then I heard my mother's voice:
"Scrub your knees."
So I bought a brand-new loofa and I let it torture me.

WHERE IS MY GREEN THUMB?

I love plants, they love me not.
A friend told me, "Talk to them,
They will respond in green."
I did.
First they turned brown,
Then they fell to the ground.

So I bought a little cactus.
A desert plant, a desert girl
As happy as can be!
But then one day
It jumped the shelf,
"Suicidal it turned to be."
That was when I faced the fact,
A green thumb I have not.

A PHONE CALL

I dial your number
To ask for instructions.
I listen to guidance
For the choices to punch.
I punch the next choice
And I'm hailed with abundance
Of more of the choices
And numbers and recorded advice.
I punch and I listen
To yet some more voices.
Then dial again
To reach some more choices.
And choices lead to even more choices.
I get disconnected.
Should I start again?
It's my choice.

CALL WAITING

I call my friend's number,
Who puts me on hold.
Call waiting has timed it
As soon as I called.
Then as I am waiting
My call waiting comes through.
I hold her call waiting
And I pick up mine too,
Disconnecting my call.
So I call back to pursue.
Thus my day goes by,
Calling and holding,
Dialing and waiting.

BABY PRESTON

Not a bundle of joy,
But joy in abundance.
You grab all attention,
Love and affection.
Heaven's angels had a message,
Their messenger, Preston.
A gift from Heaven,
A package with no instruction.
That is because
YOU ARE THE MODEL OF PERFECTION.

HARLEY

I want to ride a Harley
Or I'm going to Peru.
I want to ride a Harley
At a speed of eighty-two.
I want to ride a Harley
And be ahead of you.
And when I turn the corners
I'll be as good as you.

DEAN

Our elders asked:
"Is it a dislocated hip?
Or a bad knee?
Could it be a nerve
That lets the head swing
From shoulder to shoulder?"
"Oh no," the young women answer,
"It is the Dean imitation,
The James Dean on whom
Every modern young man
Patterns himself.
He came from the land of the famous,
Where the Cadillacs are and the Buicks,
Lincoln, Jefferson, and Truman.
It is the Dean who came from Hollywood
And our young men copied with perfection."

SHAKE

To shake or not to shake,
Hands, that is!
It was recently proven
By germatologists
That the classic greeting
Was accused of being
A rocket transporter of germs.
Never again will I hand out my arm.
It is mentally taped to my side.
No standing up for the good old handshake,
That firm and warm greeting I'm raised on.
Sometimes it is replaced by a high five.
A bow, or a smile should suffice.

A GLANCE

To avoid narcissistic behavior,
All mirrors are to be confiscated.
Had the young man refrained
From looking into the water,
Narcissism would have been eradicated.
Is it a disease not easily investigated?
Not even by immunization eliminated?

Trim the swollen ego,
Give modesty a chance.
Today you admire your YOU.
Tomorrow you won't even glance.

RECOMMENDATION

I received a recommendation
After twenty some years of anticipation,
Of thinking, planning, pondering,
And wondering about this and that.
The letter was signed, "Jesus Christ."
It described my residence on High.
It said: "On the day of judgment
You will be seated on His right,
For you have coped with the following . . ."
And here it is listed from A to Z:
In America: You lived in Wisconsin.
At Zablocki:* You earned your living.

*The name of the VA hospital in Milwaukee.

WILL

To whom it will concern:
I leave the cholesterol-free world,
The eggless omelettes and the veggie burgers.
I also leave the icy roads and laundry loads,
The crowded supermarkets, the chocolate delight,
And the eggplant Parmesan.
I leave no guilt, no bills, no maxed credit cards.
My journey is not personal nor unique,
For everyone shall join someday.
It's not a round trip but one way,
We'll gather together on different days.

DON'T TELL MARTHA

Enjoy your Prego and Ragu
Fill up your ready-made piecrust, indulge.
Your pizza-to-go, just call and order.
The golden arches, pay them a visit.
The king of burgers, don't dethrone.
Print *Wendy* on your tour map.
Then tell Martha:
The stewards served me good food
On every flight I flew.
Let her continue to cook from scratch.
As for me, I'll scratch my pans no more.

SAID MY LITTLE TOE

Crammed between the sole and the upper,
Screaming for space to stretch,
Pleading, bleeding, and threatening.
Sending electric shocks to the brain,
Demanding release, asking, "Why the severe punishment?
I am the tiniest, and shortest of them all."
BUT, OH, YOUR SCREAMS ARE THE LOUDEST OF THEM ALL.

DEATH BY DROWNING

The soft blue waters
Smile at me.
The calm, smooth waves
Invite me.
The yellow sandy shores
Comfort me.
Propelled to the depth,
I dive.
The ebb and flow
Hug me.
The aqua jets
Heal me.
I am drowning in the comfort
Of the waters.

THE NARROW ROAD

I am on a long trip,
Following every turn and bend.
First the road branches,
Then it turns and curves.
At long last the sign pointed
To a road named Honesty.
That too is on my map.
I took the turn and off I went,
I followed every twist.
It twirled to a tight spot
And I did not know
If I was heading north or south.
A challenging road, indeed, it was.
"It's west you are going,
So watch out your next step.
Better yet, just stand still,
For it may be fatal to move."
I stopped and I turned,
I took the other road.
I will come back
When I'm ready.

LUNCHEON

They came from every nation
For a luncheon celebration.

From Italy, Spain, and China,
The Middle East and Australia.

In English they are speaking.
But listen to the vibration
Of every mother's tongue dictation?!
Amusing, fascinating, enlightening, entertaining,
Their topics are as varied as their every destination.

BIRTHDAYS

They come when we're one,
Twenty-one,
Or a hundred and one.
They come on weekends
And on weekdays too.
They come when we're healthy
Or sick with the flu.
Snowstorm, rainstorm, ice storm, windstorm, any storm,
They come.
Quitting, they will.
And send us the chill.
So let's welcome their recurrence
And greet it with a thrill.

Written in Dr. Seuss's style, for grown-ups who don't like to acknowledge their birthdays.

U

Exceeded every expectation,
Leaped high above every obstacle;
Soared to heights
Not even NASA can dream of;
Achieved every level
Of hope and wish;
Touched the clouds,
The sky, and the earth.

Where are you headed?
I cannot even guess,
Because you are U.

Recipes from Egypt

Main Dishes

EGYPTIAN-FLAVORED BROTH

Ingredients:
About 1 quart water (you may need to keep adding water to have enough broth after the meat is cooked)
1 lb. beef or chicken or turkey
1 clove garlic
1 whole onion
1 cardamom seed (This can be found in Middle Eastern stores or in the spice section at most grocery stores.)
1 clove
A dash of salt

Method:
Bring water to a boil. Drop in chicken or beef, and the rest of the broth ingredients. Boil until cooked. Remove beef/chicken and set aside. Remove onion, garlic, clove and all other added spices, and discard.

Makes 4 cups (1 quart) of broth.

This broth is useful in many of the following recipes.

OKRA WITH BROTH

Ingredients:
2 bags (16 oz. each) frozen okra (sliced or whole)
1 large onion (chopped)
Salt and pepper to taste
A dash of each of the following:
garlic powder
allspice
nutmeg
1 Tbsp. lemon or lime juice
8 ozs. tomato sauce (4 ozs. tomato paste can be used)
2 Tbsp. butter, oil, or margarine
2–3 cups Egyptian-flavored chicken or beef broth (See the first recipe in this section of the book.)

Stovetop method:
In a saucepan place the oil, margarine, or butter and the minced onion. Sauté.
Add the okra and mix. Add the tomato sauce and spices. Let simmer for about 5 minutes. Stir gently. Add the broth, bring to a boil, then lower heat. Let simmer on low heat for 20 minutes or until done.
NOTE: Add more water or broth as needed to avoid too dry a dish. There should be some sauce when you serve the okra.

Oven method:
If you wish, you can bake it in the oven. After adding the broth, pour into a baking dish and bake, covered, for 20 minutes at 350°F. Check for readiness. Uncover. Bake for 10 to 15 minutes more.

Variation:
If you wish to add beef or chicken bits add them when you are sautéing the onions.

Serves 6.

MOLOKHIA
(Green Vegetable Soup)

Ingredients:
1 package frozen or dried molokhia (chopped) (This can be found in Middle Eastern stores.)
3–4 garlic cloves, minced
6 cups Egyptian-flavored beef, chicken, or turkey broth (Use a double recipe of the first recipe in this section of the book.)
1 Tbsp. vegetable oil or butter
Salt to taste

Method:
Bring the broth to a boil. Separate the chopped molokhia and drop into gently boiling broth. Do not stir.

Let boil for 3 to 4 minutes and remove from heat.

In a frying pan, heat a tablespoon of oil or butter and add the minced garlic and a dash of salt. Stir for a brief second, then pour over the molokhia soup, and cover. Serve hot.

Serves 6.

STUFFED GRAPE LEAVES

Ingredients:
8 oz. jar of preserved grapevine leaves (These can be found in the international food section of many grocery stores, or in Middle Eastern/Mediterranean stores.)
OR: 5 to 6 dozen fresh young grape leaves (This is a good springtime dish)
2 oz. butter or margarine or oil
Salt and pepper to taste
1 large onion, chopped, raw
1 cup uncooked rice, used uncooked

1½ lbs. ground beef, raw
2 cups Egyptian-flavored beef broth
1 Tbsp. tomato sauce
lemon juice to taste

Method:
If the grape leaves are jarred:
Half-fill a large pot with tapwater and bring to a boil. Drop the grape leaves into the boiling water to remove the salt. Drain immediately. Do not let them boil. Pour out the water. Place the leaves gently in a colander, to drain.

If leaves are fresh:
Let simmer till tender, then drain (about 10 minutes)

For all grape leaves:
Measure the chopped onion, salt, pepper, allspice, and oil or margarine into a bowl. Mix well. Add the tomato sauce, the uncooked rice, and raw meat to the mixture.

On a flat plate, gently spread out one grape leaf at a time, smooth side down, veined side up. (So the smooth side will end up on the outside of the rolled grape leaf.)

Put 1 Tbsp. of the filling in a line along the stem edge. Fold this edge over it, then fold both sides in toward the center and roll upward like a small cigar.

Fill the rest of the grape leaves in the same way.

Pack the leaves tightly in layers in a heavy-bottomed pan. Pour the Egyptian-flavored broth over the leaves. Cover tightly and cook over low to medium heat for 30 minutes. Uncover.

Add a half cup of Egyptian-flavored broth, mixed with one Tbsp. of lemon juice. Cover and cook for another 20 minutes.

Let them cool in the pan, then turn them over onto a serving platter. Serve with cucumber dip. (See the next recipe.)

CUCUMBER DIP
(To be served with the stuffed grape leaves)

Ingredients:
1 medium cucumber
8 ozs. sour cream or yogurt
Salt to taste
Garlic to taste—fresh or powder. If fresh, it has to be minced (creamy).
1 Tbsp. dried mint (This can be found in Middle Eastern stores or in the spice section at most grocery stores, if you don't have some from your garden.)

Method:
Wash the cucumber, and cut it into small bits. Salt lightly. Cover and refrigerate. Let stand for 10 to 20 minutes. This will bring out the excess water in the cucumber, and will keep your dip from being too watery.

While the cucumber is in the refrigerator, add garlic, salt, and mint to the sour cream or yogurt. Mix well.

Pour off the excess water from the cucumber. Add the drained cucumber bits to the sour cream. Mix well. Serve alongside stuffed grape leaves.

MOUSAKA

Ingredients:
2 large eggplants
1 small can tomato sauce (16 oz.)
1 lb. ground beef
Salt and pepper to taste
1 large onion, chopped
4 Tbsp. vegetable oil
Allspice to taste
Nutmeg to taste
Vegetable oil spray

Method:
Preheat oven to 350°F.
Cut the eggplant into slices crosswise (to make circles). Sprinkle with a little salt and let stand for 20 minutes.
Sauté the onion in a little butter or margarine. Add the ground beef, stir gently. Add the salt, pepper, allspice, and nutmeg. Stir well. Add the tomato sauce and let simmer for 10 to 15 minutes. Remove from heat.
Squeeze out excess water from the eggplant slices.
Spray a broiling pan or a sheet of aluminum foil with vegetable-oil spray. Place the eggplant on the pan or foil. Broil for approximately 10 minutes on each side, 3 to 4 inches from the broiling element.
In a baking dish, arrange one layer of eggplant, then a layer of the prepared ground beef, then a second layer of the eggplant. (The eggplant should be the top layer)
Bake uncovered at 350°F for 30 to 45 minutes.
Serve hot.

Serves 4–6.

FATTA
(Bread, rice, and meat)

Ingredients:

4–6 loaves pita bread cut into bite-size pieces (Pita bread is available at most grocery stores.)
1–2 cups Egyptian-flavored beef broth (depending on how soft you want the bread)
2 cups cooked rice
1–2 lbs. Egyptian-flavored beef stew (see below)
2 Tbsp. butter or margarine
2–3 cloves garlic (minced)
1 Tbsp. white vinegar

Egyptian-flavored beef stew:

1–2 lbs. beef stew meat, cubed
1 quart water
1 whole onion
1 cardamom seed
1 clove

Sauté beef, then simmer in the water with the spices, adjusted to taste. Simmer for 20 minutes.

Method:

Pour the broth over the cut bread to cover the surface. Let stand 5 minutes, so the broth will soak into the bread. Spread the rice over the bread. Spoon the beef stew over the rice.

To make garlic butter: Melt the butter and then add garlic. Stir gently for a minute or two over low heat. Remove from heat.

Add the white vinegar to the garlic butter, and sprinkle this mixture over the meat, rice, and bread so it drenches most of the surface.

Serve hot, right after pouring on the garlic butter.

Variation:

You can fry the bread lightly for extra taste.
You can also fry the meat lightly for extra taste, if you choose to.

Serves 6.

A traditional dish served at Christmas and Easter. See Chapter 5 for a description of the serving of this dish, and of Arab versions.

BUFTAKE
(Veal or beef cutlets)

Ingredients:
6–8 slices of boneless veal or beef cutlets (about ¼ thick)
Salt and pepper to taste
1 large onion, cut into rings
2 Tbsp. dried mint (This can be found in Middle Eastern stores or in the spice section at most grocery stores, if you don't have some from your garden.)
2 eggs, beaten
Bread crumbs
Vegetable oil to sauté in

Method:
Sprinkle the mint, salt, and pepper on the onion rings, and mix well. In any coverable dish, alternate layers of meat with the onion mix. Cover and let stand in the refrigerator for approximately 1 hour.

Beat the eggs. Pour some bread crumbs onto wax paper or onto a plate.

Prepare a frying pan for sautéing by heating the oil in the pan.

Clean the cutlets from the onion mixture as best you can. Dip the slices of meat in the beaten eggs. Then dip them in the bread crumbs to cover each side. Sauté one side until golden, then turn over to the other side for a few more minutes.

Serve on a platter decorated with such greens as parsley or lettuce. Potato chips can be used for decoration too.

Serves 6–8.

Children love this recipe, as do adults. We prepare it frequently as a treat for the family or to serve to guests.

RICE WITH NUTS

Ingredients:
2 cups white rice, cooked according to directions on the bag
1/2 cup each:
1/2 cup walnuts, chopped
1/2 pecans, chopped
1/2 pine nuts, whole
1/2 raisins, whole
NOTE: You can adjust quantities on, include, or eliminate any of these nuts, according to personal taste.
1 tsp. ground cinnamon
1/2 tsp. powdered cloves

Basic Method:
　　Add the cinnamon and cloves to the liquid while cooking the rice.
　　In a separate bowl, mix all the nuts and raisins. Lightly toast in a frying pan over medium heat. Stir while toasting, to avoid burning. Set aside.
　　Serve the nut mixture with the rice in one of the following ways:

Variations:
　　You can mix the nuts with the rice after it is completely cooked.
　　Or when rice is half cooked, add the nut mix, then turn the rice and nut mixture into a baking dish, and complete cooking by baking uncovered in a moderate (350°F) oven.
　　Another way to serve this dish is to mound the rice onto a platter, then press the nut mixture into the top of the rice.
　　You can add cooked chicken giblets to the nuts.
　　You can add cooked chicken giblets and serve with no nuts.
Serves 6–8.

This is a festive dish, usually served during feasts or parties.

MINT CHICKEN

Ingredients:
1 large chicken, cut into serving pieces (breast, wings, drumsticks, thighs). Or, if you prefer, a similar quantity of chicken, but in the pieces of your choice (breasts only, drumsticks only, ect.)
1 large onion, cut into rings
1 Tbsp. dried mint (This can be found in Middle Eastern stores or in the spice section at most grocery stores, if you don't have some from your garden.)
Salt and pepper to taste

Method:
Preheat oven to 350°F.

Sprinkle the salt, pepper, and mint onto the onion rings. Mix, pressing the onions to squeeze out some of the water. Reserve the onion liquid.

Clean the chicken as advised on wrapper. Squeeze out excess water. Add chicken to onion mix and onion liquid. Wrap tightly in plastic or place in Ziploc (or other sealable) bag. Marinate for 30 to 60 minutes in refrigerater.

Place aluminum foil in a baking dish. Arrange chicken pieces on the foil.

Cover the chicken with either foil or the baking dish's cover. Bake one hour, covered.

Uncover and let bake to desired golden color.

Serves 4–6.

Desserts

BAKLAVA

Syrup:
1 cup sugar
2 cups water
1 Tbsp. lemon juice
1 tsp. vanilla

Combine the water and the sugar in a medium saucepan. Place over medium heat, stir until the sugar dissolves. Add the lemon juice. Stir, and let simmer over low heat for 30 minutes. Let cool. Then add the vanilla. Set aside.

Filling:
1/2 cup pecans or walnuts, chopped
1/2 cup almonds, chopped, or sliced into any shape
1/2 cup raisins
1/4 cup hazelnuts (optional), chopped
NOTE: *You can include or eliminate any of these nuts, according to personal taste.*
1 Tbsp. confectioner's sugar
1 Tbsp. ground cinnamon

Prepare the filling by mixing all of the above well. Set aside.

Filo dough:
1 lb. filo dough (in the freezer section of most grocery stores, along with pastries), thawed

(Thaw filo over night in refrigerator, or for 2 to 3 hours on the counter.)

Preheat oven to 350°F.

Melt 2 sticks of butter and keep liquid, while you work with the filo dough.

Unwrap filo carefuly and divide it in half by taking the top half and separating it from the bottom half. Wrap one half in wax paper and set aside.

Assembly:

Lay the other half in a greased oven pan. 12"×16" is best, but 9"×13" is okay. Spread the filling over it. Unwrap the half of the filo dough that is in wax paper and lay it over the filling. Cut into triangular shapes.

Pour the liquid (hot) butter over all the baklava in the pan, especially between the cut slices.

Bake at 350°F for 30 minutes, or to desired golden color.

As soon as you take it out of the oven, pour the cold syrup over it. Cover the whole pan with the syrup, by tilting to each side briefly.

KONAFA

Syrup:
Same as baklava, only let it simmer an extra 10 minutes

Filling:
Same as baklava

Kataifi:
1 lb. kataifi (This shredded filo-like dough is available frozen at all Mediterranean stores: Greek, Italian, Middle Eastern)
1 lb. butter, melted

Method:
Preheat oven to 325°F.

Thaw dough. Separate and cut the shredded dough into small pieces. Mix with one pound of melted butter.

Place half the kataifi in the bottom of a round 10" or a square 8"×8" baking dish. Spread the filling over it. Add the rest of the kataifi over the filling.

With wax paper in hand, press down so that the bits of shredded dough stick together.

Bake at 325°F for 60 minutes to 90 minutes, until color is golden.

Pour the cold syrup over the hot konafa as soon as it is out of the oven.

Cut into any shape you like. Serve warm or cold.

BASBOUSSA

Syrup:
Same as baklava, only let it simmer an extra 10 minutes

Basboussa:
3 cups semolina
1 cup sugar
1¼ sticks butter or margarine, melted
½ cup milk
1 tsp. baking powder
almond halves

Method:
Mix the semolina, the sugar, and the melted butter. Add the milk and mix the dough until it holds together. You may add a tablespoon of water if the dough is too dry. Add the baking powder and mix well.

Pour into a greased 9"×13" baking dish.
Cover and let stand for 30 minutes in refrigerator.
Preheat oven to 350°F.
Cut into triangles and place half an almond on each slice.
Place in preheated oven and bake uncovered at 350°F to a pale golden color. (Approximately 30 minutes.)
Pour the cold syrup over the hot basboussa.
Can be served warm or cold. May be served with whipped cream on the side if desired.